RELEASING
God's
Life
through the
Hearts of Men

RELEASING
God's
Life
through the
Hearts of Men

DAVID CASE

CREATION
HOUSE
A STRANG COMPANY

RELEASING GOD'S LIFE by David Case
Published by Creation House
A Strang Company
600 Rinehart Road
Lake Mary, Florida 32746
www.creationhouse.com

The names in this book have been changed to preserve the anonymity of the individuals on whom the anecdotes were based.

Unless otherwise noted Scripture quotations are from the New King James Version of the Bible. Copyright © 1979, 1980, 1982 by Thomas Nelson, Inc., publishers. Used by permission.

Scripture quotations marked NAS are from the New American Standard Bible. Copyright © 1960, 1962, 1963, 1968, 1971, 1972, 1973, 1975, 1977 by the Lockman Foundation. Used by permission. (www.Lockman.org)

Scripture quotations marked TLB are from The Living Bible. Copyright © 1971. Used by permission of Tyndale House Publishers, Inc., Wheaton, IL 60189. All rights reserved.

Scripture quotations marked AMP are from the Amplified Bible. Old Testament copyright © 1965, 1987 by the Zondervan Corporation. The Amplified New Testament copyright © 1954, 1958, 1987 by the Lockman Foundation. Used by permission.

Cover design by Karen Grindley

Copyright © 2008 by David Case
All rights reserved

Library of Congress Control Number: 2008920093
International Standard Book Number: 978-1-59979-328-3

First Edition

08 09 10 11 12 — 987654321
Printed in the United States of America

CONTENTS

Introduction 1

1 Not the Picture! 5

2 Get the Picture? 15

3 Oh, Really? 25

4 Making Sense of Life 39

5 Two Targets 55

6 The Impostors 67

7 Why Brokenness? 79

8 The Real Deal 91

9 From the Image of Dust 105

10 Turning Obstacles into Pearls 115

11 The Grace Canopy 129

12 Following the Voice 143

13 Weighting for God 155

14 Steps Toward Life 173

15 Closing Access Points 187

16 Midwifing the Life 199

17 Shaping Hearts 213

Appendix 223

Notes 227

About the Author 229

INTRODUCTION

My passion as an author, and the purpose of Live Free Ministries, is to nurture the presence and power of Christ's life in the church and in its leaders. If current trends continue, the future of the church in America does not look bright. The church needs an infusion of His presence and His power.

Much of the church of today is still ministering as if to an Ozzie-and-Harriet generation. What worked in the 1950s will not work today. Our nation has changed. In the 1950s we were ministering to a nation that still had prayer and the Bible in the public school system. Everyone knew the biblical stories. Everyone had the moral baseline of the Ten Commandments. Not everyone embraced the biblical teachings, but the backdrop of the teachings was present and generally accepted as the standard for societal thinking and behavior.

Today, when the typical person under age thirty walks into a church, he (or she) is likely to know next to nothing about the Bible, and what he does know probably has negative connotations for him. The moral baseline he has been taught is likely to be some sort of self-created "Follow your own heart" morality. He will be none too quick to hand over the reins of that moral base to some outside Authority. He will be very suspicious of any demanding or dictating spiritual Authority, because he has been taught that all truth is relative and that his own experience is sufficiently authoritative for him. He does not think he needs some outside force, even if it is God, telling him what to do. In the past the church has taken for granted that the individual would respect her moral authority. That is no longer reality today.

On top of that, the prevalence of divorce and re-marriage has created turbulent family situations. Almost every person in this under-thirty, Generation Y age group that is walking into a church today has had some kind of trauma inflicted on him during his youth.

This is not clean, rock-free, weed-free soil waiting for the seed of the Word of God; however, the church of today seems to think that we can treat rocky soil as if it were a lush garden, prepared and ready to receive what God has for it.

To be effective with Generation Y and beyond, the church has to change. I believe that one of the greatest changes we will have to make will be a move toward more one-on-one coaching and mentoring activities. We can no longer depend on the "one-size-fits-all" programs that we have used over the years. We must invest in people—one person at a time. We need to identify the value and uniqueness of each person, gently and carefully nurturing that precious pearl within until it becomes the thing of beauty it was created to be.

We cannot be turned off by the outward appearance of moral decay. We must learn to see through the decadence to the purpose of God in each person. As we learn to identify and speak God's destiny for a person, we will be starting down the path of truly being a life-giver. We will be activating and releasing the life of God to flow through that person.

Discovering God's vision for a person, and then valuing that person through fellowship, are the tools needed to reach the younger generations—and these same tools are just as effective with the older generations. As the church, we must adapt or we will die. We must learn a new way of ministry, because we are ministering to a generation unlike any other we have ministered to in the history of this nation.

This book is written as a companion text to *Becoming Lifegivers*. In the appendices of *Becoming Lifegivers* there is an extended section of scriptural support and explanation for the concepts detailed in these books. In *Releasing God's Life*, there is no accompanying scriptural apologetic for the topics. Those who want the deeper theological basis for the concepts will need to read the appendix of *Becoming Lifegivers*.

Releasing God's Life is meant to lay the foundation for one-on-one ministry. It is designed to give the reader the tools he will need to better understand himself and to grow, but more importantly, to better understand others so that he can help awaken the call and purpose that God has for each individual. That is the goal of this series of books and materials—to teach people to be lifegivers in the midst of an increasingly decadent generation.

The generation of the 1950s had the moral baseline and the biblical knowledge necessary to walk into a church and respond to things being said in a positive way. Today, we are still expecting people to walk into a church, get saved, and just start living godly lives. It is not realistic. We must help them grow through the infant, toddler, child, and teen years, and that takes individual attention.

Releasing God's Life gives us a model and the tools for one-on-one ministry that can and will grow a hurting generation into men and women of God. There are no shortcuts. It is hard work, but incredibly rewarding. There is nothing like nurturing a confused and hurting spiritual child into a healthy, spiritual adult who is then able to nurture others.

This is the work of ministry, and we are all called to take part in this work. Certainly some will be called to do this in a major way and some in minor ways, but we all are called to disciple others. This is what discipleship will look like in our generation. No longer can discipleship consist of a few training courses that will put the crowning touch on a solid moral baseline. Today, we must be ready to nurture spiritual children from infancy to adulthood.

Because I believe this kind of nurturing is the work of every person in the church, I have chosen to use the third person plural of "we" as the most common point-of-view in this book. I am assuming that most of those reading this book first of all want to grow as a believer in Christ, and also desire to learn to lead others into growth in Christ. This is truly the work of "we," the body of Christ.

Are you ready to see the purpose of God released in you, and then in and through others? If you are, I believe that you will find this book to be a helpful and effective tool to move you farther down that road. May God bless you mightily as you set your face to take on the work of the kingdom in a changing world!

Chapter 1

NOT THE PICTURE!

My name is Grande." The young woman almost hissed and lurched at me as a guttural voice came out of her once delicate mouth. The tension in the air was thick, and it was clear that this demon had no intention of letting go without a fight.

In our culture, mention the spirit realm and you are likely to conjure up notions of exorcisms or witchcraft, or maybe some kind of meditation technique. Our concept of the spirit realm is like what I have just described, with demons screaming or objects moving, or a chanting person with a blank stare. However, to think of these things as the core of the spiritual realm would be like saying drug dealers and pedophiles represent who we are as a nation.

Neither exorcisms nor Eastern mysticism describe the core function of the spirit realm. In God's kingdom, the spirit realm is the source of life, health, and strength. It is the ability to have a vibrant experience with God, the power to walk away and be free from bondage, and to be released into a life of peace and joy. The bizarre encounters are the exception and not the norm.

I have only had a handful of classic encounters with the demonic in my life—encounters where you begin to pray for someone and the hissing and foaming at the mouth and guttural voices come back at you. In our culture these kinds of demonic manifestations are much less common than they are in some cultures. But that doesn't mean that we aren't in a war with the demonic realm!

Spiritual Realm Works Subtly

What this actually means is that most of the time, the workings of the spiritual realm are subtle almost to a point where many do not even acknowledge that the spirit world exists. Heaven and hell are considered fables, and angels and demons are questionable to many. It is fully possible for a person to go through life and have only a minimal number of experiences that cannot be explained without forming a belief in the spiritual realm.

Standing in the middle of a hospital lobby was not the ideal place to face a hissing, growling person. This young girl, Tara, had been experiencing an advancing paralysis along with seizures. She had bounced from doctor to doctor and hospital to hospital, only to be told that her illness was psychosomatic. Somehow the doctors had come to the conclusion that both the seizures and the paralysis were self-induced.

Seeing an extremely disheartened young lady in front of me, I reached out to pray for Tara. It was then that the fireworks hit. I have to admit, the idea that these symptoms might have been demonically induced had been in the back of my mind, but I'm not one to jump to conclusions. Considering what was coming from Tara's mouth, I didn't have to jump very far to come to the conclusion that this was a true demonic manifestation.

We write off the spiritual as the realm of the magical or the religious.

It is amazing to me that our society throws around terms like *psychosomatic illness*, for which we have no explanation and no cure, while at the same time many of these same people are unwilling to consider the possibility that the spiritual realm could be a part of the picture. We write off the spiritual realm as the magical or the religious and seem to think that it has no relevance to the life we live. Yet even science, which chooses to deal solely in the material world, ends up having to use terms like *psychosomatic illness*.

There is more to this world than can be explained through chemical reactions. Love, for example, is not merely a product of hormonal chemistry that happens according to chance encounters. It takes much more than simple chemistry to understand a human being. As the Bible describes, we are truly spiritual beings.

Even so, it is easy to completely miss the spiritual part of our nature, because the spirit realm tends to operate very subtly most of the time. What do I mean by subtle? Romans 8:16 starts us off, "The Spirit Himself bears witness with our spirit that we are children of God." Even though the Holy Spirit is a part of the Godhead and is omnipotent and omnipresent, when the Holy Spirit comes to us, He does not completely take over our spiritual activity. He comes along side and "bears witness" with our spirit. He puts Himself in the position of responding to our request at salvation and connects with our hearts. Even after salvation, we can grieve Him (see Eph. 4:30) in ways that limit His connectedness to us, or we can embrace Him more and more in a closer and more fulfilling relationship. The Holy Spirit's relationship with us is nothing like the picture from above where the demonic, upon being triggered, actually replaces normal function with its own. Given the opportunity, the demonic will occupy our spirit. The Holy Spirit takes more of a come-along-side role and acts as an influence.

A good description is a hand in a glove. The Spirit is like a glove that fits. It comes alongside the hand to protect and enhance its function. It is not very noticeable. It is subtle. There are times when a glove does not fit well and there is almost a fight between the hand and the glove. Then we notice the glove. There are times when the Spirit has a kind of fight with us, because we don't want to surrender to the will of God. We call that conviction, and we notice that work of the Spirit. Most of the time the Spirit is there renewing us, giving the believer strength, hope, peace, and joy. And we hardly notice.

It is all done very subtly. God's Spirit bears witness with our spirit. Most people hardly even notice the Spirit's work and therefore do not even have the kind of ongoing experience in their lives that clearly demonstrates to them that He exists. Learning to release the life of God into a situation is as simple as noticing and nurturing the work of the Spirit in that situation. That seems simple enough, but it is so easy to get sidetracked by the greater dramas of life.

The dramatic events of life seldom are the most important.

I did pray for Tara. The demon left. The paralysis disappeared. But the work of God had only just begun. The dramatic events of life seldom are the most important. A house cleaned and swept of the demonic is merely an invitation to trouble unless that house is continually filled with the presence of God. (See Luke 11:25.)

For Tara, the difficult issues were yet to come. She needed to deal with the superstitions that had created a continual flow of fear in her life. The fear she was experiencing gave the demonic spirits the authority to overtake Tara. Her self-pity and subsequent raging at her husband and family were the residue for Tara of behaviors the demonic spirit had energized.

Perhaps the greatest struggle was Tara's tendency to run. It is possible to see great changes in the life of an individual—if there is commitment and accountability. Those who run at the first sign of being challenged are all but impossible to help. Though it seemed like a fierce battle, and it certainly had me out on the edge of my comfort zone, the deliverance was easy compared to what followed.

Connections in the Spirit Realm

The most important issue in life for me is continually walking in the presence and under the control of the Spirit of God. We are designed to be temples of God. (See 1 Corinthians 6:19.) We are designed to connect with God's spiritual presence. We are not complete without that spiritual presence on board. God means for us to connect with His presence, but that same design also makes it possible for us to connect with the demonic.

There are those who directly seek out the demonic. These people will potentially succumb to the kind of demonic possession that Tara experienced. However, the work of the demonic does not need that level of takeover to significantly influence an individual. The primary purpose of the demonic is to keep us away from God and God's presence. If the demonic can keep us distracted with things that God will have no part of (like fear or self-pity), it can successfully complete its mission without directly taking control.

For anyone who denies that the spirits even exist, the demonic realm is able to work under cover. Demons come and connect with the evil that a person is plotting and subtly energize it. Because the person doesn't believe the demonic exists, the demons can do this work without even being noticed. The person will notice that even when he desires to do right, he often seems to be "led" into something else. But could that be the demonic? For those who do not believe that spirits even exist, their reply likely might be, "No! It can't be! It's not dramatic enough—there's no hissing, no out of control behavior! Besides, Satan isn't even real."

We Are Designed to House Spiritual Presence

Whether we knowingly invite the presence or not, we are designed to house spiritual presence. If we connect with the Spirit of God, He is much more of a gentleman. He will gently ask us to surrender area by area to the lordship of Jesus Christ until the whole house has come under His influence. At least that is the way it is meant to operate. Certainly there are times when the Spirit operates much more dramatically in and through believers, but even those claiming to walk in great spiritual power would have to acknowledge that many hours of their day are not about a dramatic spiritual manifestation.

We live in a society that is largely desensitized to the spiritual realm—whether we are talking about the Spirit of God or the demonic. We are so in touch with the material realm and so out of touch with the spirit realm that most of us have little if any clue how we are being influenced spiritually. In some ways that makes us less vulnerable to the dark spiritual realm. We don't sense it; we don't directly connect with it. We limit the influence darkness has over us to a more passive control. Accordingly, in Western culture we rarely see a person possessed by demons, such as I described earlier.

Theology of "Works"

Unfortunately, the same lack of sensitivity to the spirit realm tends to shut down our ability to connect with God's Spirit. We tend to live our Christian life from a "Do this…" or "Don't do that …" point of view, instead of being vessels for the presence of God. We have tried every kind of doctrinal gymnastic to say that what we are doing is not a works theology. The reality is that a "Do this …" theology is an attempt to work toward God.

The only way out of a works theology is truly to begin to walk in the Spirit. If we carry with us the very presence of God, and if we are releasing His energy and life into the world, it is no longer a works theology—it is grace theology. We are living empowered and strengthened by almighty God. We cannot take credit for the work if the work is initiated and established by God.

Releasing God's Life is about learning to embrace the work of the Spirit in every facet of life. God's energizing presence is the answer to our every problem. Those who are unaware of the Spirit's work occasionally stumble onto points of connectedness with the Spirit and release some of His life. It happens, and we rejoice at those "God moments."

A life lived in communion with God will produce far more for God than a life dedicated to work for God.

I do not believe the Christian walk is meant to be one of stumbling onto God occasionally. It is meant to be communion in the Spirit with Him continually; and where there is communion, we should see the fruit of communion. By fruit, I simply mean results. A life lived in communion with God will produce far more for God than a life dedicated to working for God. When we are God's partner, we produce much more fruit than when we are merely a disconnected servant.

Many will read of Tara's deliverance and miss the key point. Deliverance is just a single power activity of God. Spiritual life comes from regular communion. Tara's immediate need was for deliverance, but her future desperately needed communion with God. Releasing her from the demonic was a relatively simple thing. Teaching her to walk with God and to embrace the Spirit and His work—that was the greater battle. Moving her toward communion with God was the fight that would bear fruit for years to come.

Releasing God's Life is not so much about what we release people from as what we release them to. We release them to a walk in the Spirit. That is life. It is a battle for focus. Will we focus on God (which is worship!)? Or will we focus on self? Will we focus on the natural things of this life, thinking that is all there is? Or will we slide into fear or some other perversity and focus directly on Satan?

Those who learn to connect with the presence of God and to continually focus on Him will fulfill their purpose. Those who don't even know there is a spirit realm will struggle because they are not fully connected to God's energizing power.

This book will teach you how to cooperate with spiritual law to release God's life into the world. Many have the wrong picture. They think of the spiritual realm as being the private playground of an individual, with little or no connection to real life. The truth is that everything in the spirit realm can and will have a very real and practical manifestation in the natural world. Hebrews 11:3 reminds us that "that the universe was formed" (NIV) by that which is invisible. When we learn to release the power of the spirit realm into the natural according to God's heart, we begin to release His life into this world.

The spirit realm is consistent and substantial because it is totally governed by the character and nature of God. God's nature is solid. It is fixed. Even as we consider the law of gravity to be a fixed law, so are the laws of the spirit realm solid and immutable. And most people just think of the spirit realm as being about exorcisms and spaced out gurus in meditation—that is truly "not the picture!"

O God, I pray that the eyes of my understanding could be opened so that I may be able to comprehend with all the saints what is the width and length and depth and height of the love of Christ which is available to me in His Spirit; and that I might be filled with all the fullness of God. Amen. (Prayer based on Ephesians 1:18; 3:18–19.)

Study Guide

1. In our culture, what do people typically think of when you mention the spiritual realm? What does the chapter portray as being a more accurate picture of the spiritual realm?

2. What kinds of things made it obvious that Tara was being demonically influenced? What was the medical opinion as to Tara's problem?

3. How does the chapter illustrate the subtle way that the spirit realm operates?

4. Once freed of the demonic oppression, what were some of the "more difficult" issues that Tara would face?

5. How do those who deny the function of the spirit realm put themselves in jeopardy of coming under the control of the demonic?

6. In what way does denying the spirit realm actually work to protect people from demonic influence? What are these people missing out on through this belief system?

7. What new insights have you gained about what it might mean to walk in the Spirit? What does the phrase "communion with God" mean to you and how do you cultivate it?

Chapter 2

GET THE PICTURE?

Tara's story illustrates the common view of the spiritual realm: it is spooky, magical, uncontrollable, and best left at a distance. Why would we want to connect with something that might open us up to being controlled by "Grande"?

That is the wrong picture. In fact, the word *picture* is a great start toward a better understanding of the spiritual realm. What we see on a computer screen is a picture. The picture does not give us an understanding of what a computer is or does. It is a momentary image that is being formed by a machine that is very complex and is capable of producing all kinds of visual graphics on a screen.

At any given moment, what we see in a person is a snapshot. It is a two-dimensional expression of a much more complex person who is capable of producing many different thoughts and behaviors. In a computer we know that the programming and the hard drive are generating the picture. So what generates behavior in people?

Matthew 12:34 tells us where the human response comes from, "For out of the abundance of the heart the mouth speaks." I love the phrasing of this verse: it is "out of the abundance of the heart" that the "mouth speaks." In the same way that a computer accesses a particular part of the programming on the hard drive and then responds, a person accesses a particular part of the heart, thus producing a life response.

Spiritual Presence and Spiritual Substance

There are two terms that I use to describe the function of the heart: spiritual presence and spiritual substance. Spiritual presence is more like the picture, what we would see on a screen of a computer. It is the instantaneous *now* of a person. Spiritual substance is more like the programming on the hard drive of the computer. It is the internal stuff that will ultimately determine what shows up on the screen.

As human beings we are designed to house spiritual presence, much like a radio is designed to receive radio waves being broadcast from a station. The station we tune to will determine the music we play. There are times a radio can be between stations, which produces a confusing mixture of content and static that is pure frustration to all. Like a radio, we tend to connect with one frequency or another.

We were designed to be continually connected with God's Spirit.

We were designed to be continually connected with God's Spirit. Like a television needing an input signal, we are not complete without a connecting and animating spiritual presence. Our spiritual presence is like the signal we tune to. We can tune our picture to faith (a positive spiritual presence), or we can change channels to unbelief (a negative spiritual presence). Both are available from our programming. The current spiritual presence of a person is a major part of the picture, but it is only a snapshot. It is not the entire picture.

Spiritual Recordings

Digital age technology provides us with a great illustration of how we are intended to function. With the click of a button, we can record video into a recorded storehouse to be watched at the convenience of the viewer. The recordings we carry around with us are similar to our spiritual substance. They are the programming on our hard drive.

16

Spiritual presence is the signal we are currently tuned to and playing, but spiritual substance is the stuff that gets recorded onto our digital recorder. Once something is recorded, it is always available to be accessed, usually at the point of some spiritual trigger.

Over time the stuff that is recorded in our storehouse tends to dominate what will be played for our viewing. As our databank is filled, our substance is firmly established. A new recording cannot happen unless the old recordings are overwritten. There is no room. Once this happens, current viewing tends to be dominated by the old favorites. In the same way, a person's current spiritual presence begins to be dominated by the recorded favorites over time.

God has designed us so that we have a great deal of control over what spiritual presence will be playing in our lives. Tara is the exception. Most people are not controlled by a "Grande" type of spirit. Yet, in our culture, most people are not even aware there is such a thing as a spiritual presence.

Blindness to spiritual forces actually leads to being controlled by those forces.

We all have seen cartoons depicting an angel on one shoulder and a demon on the other. If there are truly angels and demons, and if they can connect with us at a spiritual level, perhaps we are more controlled than we realize. No, we are not at the robot level that Tara was, but blindness to spiritual forces actually leads to being controlled by those forces. Imagine a person who did not know there were any controls on the video: no "on" controls, no "off" button— just a continual feed of a picture not chosen. What a life! Those who do not see and understand the workings of the spiritual realm are like that. Because we are "heart" creatures, those who cannot see how the heart functions are at the mercy of whatever triggers their heart. Even as Ephesians 6 warns us to be alert to spiritual warfare and to learn to stand against our spiritual enemy, we must learn to see beyond the natural realm. Spiritual transformation begins with learning to see the spiritual flows that influence our lives.

Multiple Layers of Negative Recordings

If a person has multiple layers of negative recording, walking him to victory can be quite a task. An example of this was Cindy, who struggled with a sense of self-condemnation. After sharing with her some of these concepts of spiritual recordings written on the heart, I began to pray for the general area of self-hatred. It was pretty clear that self-hatred was her current snapshot.

I was not quite prepared for what followed. It was as if Satan unleashed a machine gun firing of negative presences. After the initial prayers for the self-hatred area, hopelessness surfaced followed by unbelief, and then a bitter anger. It was one thing after another, and quite the fight to get her to a point of being able to rest in the presence of Christ.

I have found that when there is self-hatred or self-condemnation, it is not uncommon to have to deal with multiple issues and presences at once. These demonic presences always seem to travel in clans. Instead of dealing with a single snapshot at a time, we have to deal with the whole family album! Any attempt at ministry can quickly go sour, as words that are meant to help instead activate self-pity, hopelessness, or some other "I will never get it right" attitude.

As human beings, we tend to respond according to what is being activated in our hearts. Words or events are the trigger points that activate different files in our hearts. Science has demonstrated that there are neuro-pathways that develop in the brain that become the track on which we run. Once a person develops a self-hatred pathway, it is much easier for him to follow that path than to blaze a new trail. Thus, words that should not necessarily activate self-hatred become trigger points for self-hatred because it is the easiest pathway for the brain activity to follow. Soon, more and more activity tends to follow a few familiar trails.

When ministering to a person with self-hatred, you might say something like, "You can't do that. You can't let those kind of thoughts rule you." These words are meant to encourage the person to rise up and fight off the self-hatred, but if the person is responding from inside the spiritual hatred file, he will think, "You're right. I'm stupid and I'm weak." Instead of helping the person with your words of "encouragement," you actually trigger (or re-activate) the self-hatred file and reinforce what is already written.

People who allow these self-hatred cousins a place in their spiritual presence generally end up meditating on negative self-thoughts, thus engraving these negative patterns deep into the substance of the person. Once a presence is burned deeply into a person's substance, it is much more difficult to help the person gain a complete and lasting deliverance. And the potential life triggers to set off that negative substance are everywhere, because the person has developed a worldview that sees hopelessness at every turn. This hopelessness blocks out the presence of God and leaves even the believer with little or no ability to sense the Holy Spirit's willingness to help the person overcome his bondage.

The only solution is to get these people to see their spiritual flow of self-hatred and to recognize that this flow is leaving them isolated from the help that God is freely offering. They need to get outside of the thought flow long enough to see their spiritual flow. Once they develop a worldview that understands that we are spiritual beings, and that Satan loves to invade our temple and dominate our spiritual presence with self-hatred, they can begin to war against the enemy instead of falling into self-hatred. If we don't realize that we are being influenced by the demonic, this is not an option. But at the same time, if we don't recognize our part of giving place to the enemy, we don't own our own sin in a way that will allow us to reach the point of victory. Sin begins with a trigger point in our own hearts, but then is strengthened and escalates to a point of bondage by the power of the enemy.

Cindy had been prayed for on previous occasions. In fact, some of her deepest hurts had come through betrayal in a religious context. Accordingly, it is not surprising that prayer ended up being a trigger for her, causing other negatives to surface, one right after another. In past situations, Cindy had not been able to break through to victory, and thus prayer was just another trigger for her sense of being a failure. By recognizing the successive negative presences, and dealing with them one-by-one, we were able to break that pattern, helping Cindy return to an active sense of the presence of God. Cindy saw that much of her "failure" spiritually was just a more complex attack of the enemy, using the self-condemnation recorded in her spiritual substance as a trigger.

The Spirit Realm Dictates Life's Outcomes

Hopefully, by now you are beginning to "get the picture" of what I mean when I talk about the spirit of a man and the spiritual realm. Our society calls it attitude, and in sports we call it momentum. There is an intangible something that seems to dictate the outcomes of life; that intangible something is the spirit realm and it is governed by very clear spiritual laws.

What is written on our hearts will determine what gets played in our daily lives. Truly, out of the "abundance of the heart," the "mouth speaks" (Luke 6:45). A spiritual flow, like self-pity, gets written on the heart. A life event triggers that heart attitude. The mouth speaks forth that attitude with an incredible variety of words.

The major programming of our hearts is not words . . . but the spiritual flows tied to the words.

As a culture, we have focused on the words. We have tried to change thinking so that the words would change. We have missed the fact that spiritual flows tend to determine our thinking and thus our words. The major programming of our hearts is not a databank of words. It is the pathways that the words follow and the spiritual flows that are tied to the words.

If a person is flowing in self-pity, the words do not really matter. The demonic is right there to energize self-pity and to keep it the dominant flow, whether the person realizes he is connecting to a spiritual energy or not. The receiving tower is on and active. We are designed to house spiritual presence, and we cannot help but connect with either God's Spirit or the demonic. It will happen.

Every set of words carries a spiritual flow with it. Ephesians 4:23 tells us to be "renewed in the spirit of your mind." Our society doesn't understand the "spirit" part of that statement, so we just ignore it. In most cases the spiritual flow animating the thought is far more important than the actual words themselves.

We have been a society that analyzes content of thinking, and we have missed the animating flows. Proverbs 4:23 tells us, "Watch over your heart with all diligence, for from it flow the springs of life" (NAS). Certainly, we are to watch our words, but there is a much more important thing to watch. It is the flow of our hearts.

About the best language our society has to give us on this subject is the word *attitude*. Attitude is woefully inadequate to describe the power of spiritual flows. The word *attitude* gives us a picture of something temporal and short term. Spiritual flows like self-hatred take up residence in generation after generation and so do other flows such as bitterness or spiritual pride. Thankfully, positive flows like diligence and thankfulness are also written on the hearts of successive generations.

We have tried to teach people to change their words, not even acknowledging that those words were being animated by deeply rooted spiritual substances written on the heart. The code written on the heart activates a spiritual flow, which then connects with and is energized by the demonic. (Or by the Spirit of God!) We tell people to just "change," but we don't even know what we are asking. And we don't know how to teach them to recognize and cooperate with the spiritual realm. All we produce in others with this approach is frustration.

Teaching people to connect with the Spirit of God produces a much better result. Connecting with God is simple; we simply must recognize when we are in a bad spiritual flow, such as hatred. We then need to confess that we are accessing and housing the wrong spiritual flow. Finally, we ask God to come and connect with us and to change that flow.

This book is mostly about taking those simple steps and beginning to apply them to all life situations. What springs from the heart will determine the outcomes of life. We need to learn to see it. We need to guard and guide it. Unfortunately, all we've seen are words and actions—it is time we start seeing the heart.

Animated films were perfected by taking a number of still pictures and filming them in rapid succession. The end result was a very lifelike film with moving characters. But the film was actually an illusion. The reality was the still shots. In a way, we too are a series of still shots: a file is accessed and a picture comes forth on the screen. The picture that comes forth on the screen seems to be the whole picture, but it is not. It is one still shot of one small aspect of the heart. To change lives we must be able to see a whole heart transformed, not just activating a single still shot.

Ministering to hearts is not as simple as getting a person to repeat a few words or even to produce a few good behaviors. It is a radical and complete transformation of all that is within a person into the very image and nature of God. That is hard work, but it is very rewarding work. It is work that will help others change the programming on the inside and not just the snapshot that is showing up on the outside. This is what it means to be spiritually transformed.

Do you "get the picture"?

> *O Lord God, teach me that apart from You I can do nothing. Teach me that in You is life and godliness. In You, I have all I need to become like You and to help others do the same. Amen. (Prayer based on John 15:5; 2 Peter 1:3.)*

Study Guide

1. What part of our spiritual function does this chapter say is like a snapshot? Describe some different spiritual snapshots that might appear on your screen.

2. Just as a television or a radio requires a signal to produce programming, our spiritual flow is our animating force. In your own words, describe a spiritual force that has animated your words or actions in the last few days.

3. When you think of having a digital recorder to record spiritual impressions, what kinds of things do you believe were recorded on your recorder during the early years? Are those early recordings still having an impact? If so, how do you think they are affecting you?

4. It is possible to have multiple layers of recordings, some of which are very different. Describe some contrasting recordings that could be recorded in your spiritual substance.

5. How had prayer become a negative trigger for Cindy?

6. Why is telling a person to change their thought patterns an inadequate answer in many cases? What can we do that would be more effective?

7. What kinds of spiritual flows come out of your heart on a consistent basis? How many of them are animated by and connected to God's Spirit? How many of them cater to your selfish wants and thus connect you with a demonic flow?

Chapter 3

OH, REALLY?

Jimmy is typical of many that I have ministered to. He had no childhood issues and to suggest that he did was close to picking a fight. Everything was pretty much normal in his family and that was that.

Oh, really?

Jimmy had been saved for almost ten years when I came into the picture, and in so many ways he was a model Christian. At least it seemed that way to those in the church. He was the first to volunteer to mow the lawn, first at church on Sunday mornings. He was a Sunday school teacher. He was always faithful, always present for every service, and almost never revealed a visible flaw. But something wasn't quite right. Occasionally, a flicker of rage would peek through his calm demeanor, usually showing up when there was the cover of "righteous anger." Someone had violated God's law, and he for one wouldn't put up with it!

Jimmy had been walking in this outward righteousness for years, but the strain was about to make him crack. Rather than show his real side, he just disappeared from the church for several months. No one could believe it. No one could understand it.

Of course, Jimmy's childhood had nothing to do with it. His childhood had been "normal." His mom had cheated on his dad. At one point, his dad had pulled a gun on her. Fortunately, no shots were fired. His dad couldn't hold a job and there was constant stress and many moves. And one other minor detail—he had been molested. But, of course, he had a "normal childhood."

Oh, the games we play! For Jimmy, church had been one of those games. He thought that if he could play it long enough and well enough, that what was inside him would change—the darkness would go away. After ten years of play-acting, he began to lose hope that he could keep his performance going.

Healing finally came for Jimmy when he cracked. That's not the way we think it should happen. We think that as we grow things just go away. We gradually get it together. But real growth only happens when we truly begin to face who we are; when we start to see all the lines of stuff recorded on our spiritual hard drive. For Jimmy, that was an agonizing process. He didn't want anyone else to see his garbage. And who would?

He was literally writhing in pain physically before he finally broke and asked for help. But as is often the case, the source of the pain was more spiritual than physical. It was as if the yuck of the molestation was an internal boil that welled up inside and burst.

We are like that as human beings. One part affects the next. We are an integrated whole. The spiritual realm is always a factor in our lives in some way. For Jimmy, when we siphoned off the festering sore of the molestation, the physical symptoms faded away almost immediately. Transformation began, not because of years of being good, but after he finally began to bring the darkness of his younger years into the light. Jesus is the Light, and the Light destroys all darkness!

A Deeper Target for Ministry: Our Spiritual Substance

In order to better minister to people, we need to learn more about this deeper target of ministry: those things written on our hearts over the years. I call the lines of writing on our spiritual hard drive our spiritual substance.

The terms *personality* or *character* are about as close to the concept of spiritual substance as our society gets. If we fully ascribe to our current concepts of character or personality, modern science still has a significant problem. How does our character form? And how is it shaped so early in life? Scientists tell us that the child's personality is mostly formed by age one. Science usually tries to say that it is the brain that determines personality, but thinking skills are not even developed at age one. How can personality be so fully developed in a brain that is not even capable of any complex thinking skills?

The idea that a child's personality is developed early lines up well with a biblical model. Psalm 139:13 indicates that God forms the "inward parts" first and then covers those inward parts with a physical body. God gives each created being a unique personality as a starting point. He breathes it into existence.

Once formed, we have immediate spiritual function. Our spiritual recorder is on in the womb, and we are already recording and responding to our spiritual environment and even making spiritual choices of what presence we will connect with among those present in our world. No, we are not thinking beings to any great degree, but we are spiritual beings, bonding with the spiritual flows of parents or siblings or other significant persons.

Even as a television can pick up an external signal, babies still in the womb begin to pick up the spiritual flows of parents and of the environment around them. The recording has already begun. I am not talking about the recording of thoughts. I am talking about the recording of spiritual flows.

In John 7:38–39, Jesus gives us a picture of what I mean by spiritual flows: "He who believes in Me, as the Scripture has said, out of his heart will flow rivers of living water. But this He spoke concerning the Spirit, whom those believing in Him would receive; for the Holy Spirit was not yet given, because Jesus was not yet glorified."

God has designed us to be temples of His spiritual presence. We are designed so that our spirits can connect with the Holy Spirit, and then the two together are meant to flow out of our hearts in a life-giving flow to other people. Love is supposed to flow out of our hearts, or peace or joy, and is meant to be animated by the power of the Holy Spirit. However, this same design allows us to connect with spiritual flows in general, whether that flow is coming from another person, or even from a demonic source.

In a baby, the spirit is God breathed and is fully functioning from the beginning. Like a television, designed to receive a signal and to play programming, the spirit of the baby is searching to connect with some kind of signal, some kind of spiritual flow. If there is self-hatred flowing in the heart of the mother, it begins to knock on the door of the heart of the child. If the child connects with that flow, the empty recorder of the child will be quick to record just about anything that flows his way.

> *A child will be quick to record just about anything that flows his way.*

Yes, as human beings, we are not just capable of playing programs, but we have the ability to record those programs also. If there is peace flowing, we will likely record that peace into the spiritual databank that I call our spiritual substance. If we connect with bitterness, we will likely record that bitterness. If we connect with love, we will likely record that love. The spiritual presence we record then begins to shape our substance while still in the womb.

Again, this is spiritual function, not mental function. Even as a very small baby, we connect with a spiritual presence and then give that presence "air time." It flows through us. Even a one-month-old child clearly has times of a peaceful presence and of aggravation. He can be joyful or full of rage.

Some try to say that this early functioning of the child is governed by the subconscious mind. Others call it intuition or instinct. Scientists know that the function is there but don't know what to do with it in the current model. We have all kinds of names for things that happen outside of a conscious thinking level, but the scientific truth is that there is some kind of functioning happening very early.

I believe it is more accurate to say that we are designed as spiritual beings, capable of connecting with spiritual presence, which then flows through us. Unlike a television, even early on, we have some power over what spiritual flows we choose to connect with and which ones we record. We are God-breathed (Eccl. 12:7) and functioning spiritually from the beginning. We have a personality that is already embracing flows or rejecting flows.

In Genesis 25, the Bible describes Jacob and Esau as fighting in their mother's womb. Both children were already manifesting their unique personalities that would be lived out in so many ways over the years. In the early stages of our lives, our tiny bodies are barely capable of expressing the spiritual flows we choose to connect with, but we still are functioning individuals. Rebekah learned that. Her two children could not even get along with each other in the womb! An identical environment did not produce identical children. We are God breathed and functioning from the beginning.

Spiritual Imprints Begin at Conception

Most of the events of ages earlier than five predate significant language formation and also generally seem to predate the ability to recall these events. If thinking skills are what make us what we are, how can this be so? I believe that spiritual imprints are the most formative. If we have a functioning spirit from the very beginning, it makes sense that our recorders are beginning to fill up from the beginning.

If this is true, it also makes sense that most people are currently struggling with spiritual imprints that are completely outside of their reasoning skills or memory. As human beings, the spiritual imprint recorder reaches its full level before there is any significant ability to reason. New recordings then begin to be dictated by previously recorded imprints even before there is any sense of making any mental choices. In a sense, we do make choices. Our spirit chooses to connect or not to connect to a spiritual flow.

With each "choice," an imprinting of the heart takes place and a worldview is beginning to form, even before any thinking skills are in place. A worldview is forming because these recorded spiritual flows radically shape the thinking of the developing child. We think according to who we are, and who we are is shaped by our recorded spiritual flows.

For Jimmy, one of the flows written on his heart could be described as a fierce family loyalty. An unwritten rule of his upbringing was, "We are family. We stick together." An honest survey of childhood issues felt more like an outright betrayal to Jimmy. His substance had

programmed him to keep his mouth shut; "You don't criticize family."
He followed that programming well for years, even after he was
saved, and it nearly destroyed him. For Jimmy, there seemed to be
only one alternative: put on a good performance in Christ. It worked
for a while, but God's solution is not to hide our stuff, but to bring it
out into the open. Psalm 32:3–5 tells us:

> When I kept silent, my bones grew old
> Through my groaning all the day long.
> For day and night Your hand was heavy upon me;
> My vitality was turned into the drought of summer.
> Selah
> I acknowledged my sin to You,
> And my iniquity I have not hidden.
> I said, "I will confess my transgressions to the LORD,"
> And You forgave the iniquity of my sin.

Jimmy was shown how to live these verses. He went from groaning
to freedom; from suppression of truth to confession; from pain to
healing.

When we start to see the power of the formative years, it changes
how we minister to people. If we had the ability to see into the heart,
I believe we could trace many of the spiritual patterns of adult life all
the way back to ages earlier than five, and in many cases even to the
womb. If we could track it, I believe that we would see a great deal of
spiritual parallel between age-three recordings and adult problems
in marriage relationships. When insecurity is being recorded at age
two, insecurity becomes a major problem in a marriage relationship.
If fear and trauma settle in at age one, fear and trauma will shut down
the person's ability to function on a job.

We don't like this kind of theory because it takes us outside of the
conscious realm, and we think it takes us outside of the ability to do
anything about our future. This is not true. Actually, it is much easier
to minister to people once we realize the spiritual consistency that is
likely to be present throughout their lives.

Once we learn not to focus on the details or persons involved
in the events and look for the spiritual imprints written into our

substance, we can usually find consistency between childhood, teen years, and adult years. For example, bitterness and jealousy are prevalent. Perhaps they derive from self-hatred or arrogance. On the other hand, it is great when it is godly substance that dominates a person. That is what makes a healthy person healthy.

When we stop looking for events and start looking for substance, the spiritual imprints that dominate our digital recorder, we find what needs to be ministered to. The events in and of themselves are not the issue. They are merely imprints, the spiritual tag that goes with the event. The same car accident can generate an imprint of panic in one person, and praise for God's protection in another. As spiritual beings, it is the spiritual tag that will dominate our future responses.

We find where to minister when we look for spiritual substance.

The need is not so much to find all of the events and "think through" them. Rather, the need is to get the person to realize that the spiritual response has been consistent from childhood. In a few cases, a traumatic event can significantly change the imprints of a person, but in most cases, basic imprints tend to be consistent, many times not just for a single lifetime, but for generations. A mother (or father!) who is fearful exposes the child to that same spiritual flow of fear, which is frequently embraced by the child and incorporated into his heart. The mother that is full of joy and peace also passes that influence on to the child. The influence of the spirit realm truly goes way beyond the experiences we are capable of remembering.

Many have tried to treat this reality of generational influence as if it could be waved off with a simple prayer. If there is a single traumatic event or some kind of negative covenant made with the devil in the history of the family, the right kind of confession prayer can start a process of turn around that is very significant. As some have called it, a "generational curse" can be broken, leaving an individual with a much greater sense of freedom spiritually. However, to treat the idea of spiritual heritage as if it were something that could be changed with a few prayers is to grossly underestimate how core it is to our being.

Our spiritual substance is the deepest part of us. It is our heart. The recordings on our heart are written over a period of years and deeply inscribed A significant part of that heart is the influence from the generations, but the specific spiritual tags that we record tend to be dictated by what we value—by our own uniquely created heart given by God. Because these tags are so tightly woven into our being, the idea that we can say a few prayers and have it all go away is unrealistic. It doesn't understand the abiding power of the spiritual realm, nor cooperate with spiritual law in a way that can bring change.

Rewriting With Godly Substance

For a person to change, he must recognize the layered effect of years of spiritual substance that have been written on his heart and learn to cooperate with God to overwrite the negative recordings. While dealing with specific memories helps overwrite negative substance, it is not necessary to go back and find every memory. That would be impossible. What we need to do is recognize the general layers of negative substance and call on the Lord to help us rewrite those substances. Once the core parts of our heart have been rewritten, it creates a new pattern of seeing, which in turn changes the spiritual tags that we tend to record on our hearts from that point forward. Again, the key is recognizing current spiritual flows and substances, and seeing them changed into the image of God. The key is not erasing and rewriting every event that has ever happened.

A person who comes from a generation of self-haters will likely have self-hatred written on his heart. As the mind of that child is beginning to form, that spiritual substance is already there shaping the thinking of that child. Even at age two, a child with that kind of substance will see a stranger as threatening. He will shrink back, which will likely affect the response of the other person. The other person, not wanting to scare the child, draws away from the child. The child notices that the stranger pulls away from him, which reinforces the recording of self-hatred: "This person is pulling back and away from me. He must not think that I am very likeable."

Notice how both the life events and then the thinking are incredibly impacted by the substance of very young children. Even a little child helps generate the responses that will come his way, because of the substance that has already been recorded. Because we are so focused on thinking ability, we have not understood how early the recording process begins, nor have we understood that the most significant recordings are spiritual in nature and not governed by thoughts. Especially at this early stage of life, the spiritual governs the thoughts more than the thoughts govern the spiritual.

We must learn to recognize emerging substances that are ungodly, embrace the presence of God in its place, and overwrite the old with the new. Dealing with memories can be a helpful part of that, but the most important day is today. It doesn't matter where a negative imprint came from if I am choosing to overwrite that imprint with the stuff of God. If I have to go back and forgive a person to go on, I need to go back. But what is most important is that I go on, not that I go back!

Whatever It Takes to Move Forward!

For Jimmy, it was very helpful to go back to some of the traumatic imprints and pray through to forgiveness. For Cindy, there was almost no discussion of the events that might have caused her cluster of self-hatred presences. We simply focused on what was surfacing in the present. Having dealt with the current spiritual presence, there was a great change in Cindy. Yet for Cindy, the more important point was to realize that a current presence was not a temporal thing. It was coming out of multiple recordings on her heart. That meant she could expect the same kind of thing to surface again and again.

When she would face it again in the future, it was not to be a point of despair, but a simple recognition that not all of her substance is yet transformed. In the past, every time something negative had been triggered, she had felt like a failure all over again and had slipped back into a self-condemning mode, which simply reinforced the negative substance of her heart.

For a person to be spiritually transformed, there must eventually be a rewriting of the person's recorded storehouse. This takes a long period of time because there is an incredible amount of data recorded in our storehouse, and none of it can be overwritten without the specific permission of the individual. Also, it cannot be overwritten for good unless the person is currently accessing good programming.

As individuals of habit, we tend to access what we are used to watching. Those used to watching garbage will tend to continue to access garbage, which means that they will continue to overwrite garbage with garbage. But, we *do have* the ability to choose whether we overwrite, and what we overwrite with. (Which is to say, the imprint of the event.) But we cannot write something into our hearts that is not being accessed by our hearts. This means that we must be in touch with God's Spirit presence to have that presence written on our hearts.

For both Jimmy and Cindy, the negative inscriptions were written all over their storehouses. For Jimmy, the negative inscription was one of shame and hiding. For Cindy, it was one of continual failure. Even while they were temporarily accessing the presence of God, the negative recordings would try to creep in, telling them that they would never make it with God. When they allowed those recordings to continue playing for any period of time, the negative substance would soon vanquish the presence of God, leaving them in a state of seeking God, but not really having His presence.

The Necessity and Limitation of Healing Prayer

Unless we have access to godly spiritual presence, all we can do is recycle one of the substances within us. There must be a current connection to God's presence for healing and growth. Frequently, some sort of healing, forgiveness, or deliverance prayer is needed to get the person to a point of sensing the presence of God. Spiritual blockages must be removed to give the person the potential of connecting with godly presence. These prayers don't guarantee that the person will connect, nor do they guarantee that the person will stay connected even if there is a breakthrough. But at least they open up the possibility of connecting with God. A person with a huge area of bondage has little possibility of connecting with God without some sort of breakthrough.

Rejecting Love and Life

Again, healing and deliverance prayers *do not guarantee* what will be recorded in the storehouse. Within seconds of experiencing spiritual relief, it is possible for a person to discard the experience, to refuse the download to his storehouse. Even though it was a godly presence, he interprets it to be something of no value to himself or he may even interpret it as the enemy.

Once a person determines that a particular imprint is not something he wants recorded into his storehouse, he will revert to his years of familiar substance. This is not a conscious choice. This is a spiritual choice much like the choices made in the sub-five-year-old. This "choice" is better described as a presence he "chooses" to connect with and then download. He may actually think he is choosing one thing with his mind, but the spiritual choice will be apparent.

Many times, intercessors are totally confounded when a person whom they thought they had helped turns on them. Once the old substance reasserts itself, the person can and often will throw out the new experience, even though it was an experience of great peace and joy. If the person rejects the experience, he will also reject the person bringing the experience. He has to. As spiritual beings, we must live with some spiritual consistency, even if there seems to be absolutely no logic to it.

Too often, we play games with our minds. We think our childhood was normal. We think we have completely forgiven all our hurts and those who hurt us. We think we are walking in faithfulness. The spiritual reality is often very different. Jimmy appeared to be the model Christian for years. He forced himself to think Christian thoughts during those years, but he was not transformed through forcing himself to behave better.

An intercessor easily can be confused by the Jimmy's of the world. They see someone improving and think they are seeing growth. But sometimes they are seeing growth and sometimes they are not. It depends on what is happening in the heart of the person. Trust was a major issue for Jimmy, so he put on a show of good Christian behavior because he could not trust others to love him for who he was. When he dropped out of church, that, too, was because he could not trust people. Both the molestation and the generational flow had done some deep writing on his heart.

Healing and deliverance prayers do not guarantee what will be recorded in the storehouse.

If an intercessor gets too caught up in outward behavior, he will be blown away by the negative turns that are bound to come when working with someone who has major issues. Even the people hurting the most can outwardly get it together for a season. They are some of the best candidates for a dramatic touch of God's presence. When that happens, it seems like everything should change, but often there is no permanent download.

In Jimmy's case, he finally broke—but in breaking, he was fixed. No, it was not an immediate fix. It took years to rewrite the code, but he connected with the presence of God like he had never connected before. The love of God, accepting him for who he was—even as a sinner—began rewriting the code. He was able to put away the performance and embrace the work of God in his heart month after month and year after year.

It was not a smooth path. There were many crises along the way. He almost bailed several times. But our God is faithful. He never gave up, and He always managed to pull Jimmy back to Himself. God is truly the Source of life and the Answer to our every need.

You might be thinking, "I'm not like Jimmy. I actually *did* have a normal childhood." Oh, really? There is no fear, no lust, no selfish ambition, no shame, no jealousy, and no rebellion in your life or the life of your family? We all have lines of code, internal programming that needs to be rewritten, and much of it even predates our own ability to remember.

I was one of those good kids with a two-parent home and a normal life. I was saved at a young age and never walked away to any great degree, but I have baggage. I have struggled with self-pity and pride. I have a shame code within, and hints of rebellion.

Shall I go on?

Yeah, I'm pretty much normal. I can't see that I have any great problems—at least that was what I thought before God began to deal with me. We all tend to think our own heart is normal, because the heart is good at rationalizing life events. For those who think they have no heart issues, I have a simple question—*Really?*

> *O Lord, help me to see the lines and the precepts that have been written on my heart that are not of You. I realize that until I allow You to write Your lines and Your precepts on my heart, I am not as far along in the knowledge of You as I thought I was. God, renew the foundations of my heart! (Prayer based on Isaiah 28:9-10.)*

Study Guide

1. Many people judge Christians by their outward performance. How does Jimmy illustrate the need to look beyond the outward performance? Do you have any personal illustrations that would make this point?

2. When is good behavior an indication that a person has conquered an area? When would it not be an indicator of victory?

3. Where does this chapter suggest that character begins? How is this different from what most science today would teach? Is there factual information that would support this point of view?

4. Why would people struggle with issues that are outside of their memory or normal reasoning ability? If it is outside of memory, how can it affect that person?

5. What was an unwritten rule that controlled the way Jimmy thought and acted? How did that rule work against his ability to receive healing?

6. What are some imprints that might be written on the heart of an individual? Why do major imprints tend to last for generations?

7. Even if a person is significantly touched by God, there is no guarantee of long-term improvement. What determines where a person will end up spiritually?

Chapter 4

MAKING SENSE OF LIFE

Mary did not get it. It seemed like the whole world hated her—or at least were determined to taunt her and belittle her. Her whole life had been filled with a sense of being unloved. She was an unwanted child, the cause for a shotgun wedding and though her parents did not openly say so, it was as if they were determined to never let her forget it.

As the years went by, she became more hostile and more critical. The more she was provoked, the more she hardened her heart. The harder her heart, the sharper her words became until the law of sowing and reaping was about to destroy her. It was as if everyone in her life was taking aim with their words, hoping to leave a mark of pain. When she finally came to me, she was miserable and without hope. Life made no sense.

Words and actions, thoughts and feelings—they can all be so confusing because they so easily contradict each other. I have found that when we can see past these outward expressions and see the flows of the heart, life begins to make sense. A bitter person can only respond in ways consistent with his bitterness. Outwardly, he may be sweet one moment and ugly the next, but the spiritual flow is the key to both actions. Those who see only words and actions are puzzled. Those who learn to see the heart hold the key to making sense of life.

Mary had spent many years in church and it seemed to make no difference. When she tried to respond better to a situation, she still would get harsh words back at her. She would try to forgive, but the flood of negative thoughts she was battling would hijack her heart with the first negative comment from a friend or a family member. If going to church could not help her, what could? The first thing I began to teach her was to see the flows of her own heart.

The Beatitudes: Beginning to See Spiritual Flows

One of the best ways to get a handle on the spiritual flows of the heart is to take a look at some examples. The Sermon on the Mount lists seven positive spiritual flows. It starts with "blessed are the poor in spirit" (Matt. 5:3), and continues with spiritual flows like mourning, meekness, hunger for righteousness, mercy, purity of heart, and the peacemakers. These are positive heart flows.

Most of us have some sense of what meekness or mercy look like. The poor in spirit and mourning are a little tougher to understand. The poor in spirit are those who have reached the end of their rope. There is no pride left. They are willing to accept help from others, because they have realized their need for God.

A person whose heart is poor in spirit has an open heart. He has learned that the skills he has are not enough to handle life, and that he needs God to help him. Spiritually, he has his hands held out saying, "Please, help me!" In the Book of Judges, even when evil people would begin to plead with God, the heart of God would relent and send help. (See Judges 2:16–19.) Over and over God does this even for people not fully in repentance. Why? Because the heart of God is moved toward those who are poor in spirit—those who have recognized that they are not adequate in and of themselves, and therefore admit they need His help.

The heart of God is also moved by those who mourn. The only alternative to mourning is for us to harden our hearts. We cannot continually live in pain. We will either shut down, operate in some form of defense mechanism, or we will process our pain. Only those who choose to process their pain have a heart that is open to God. God would like to help anyone who is in pain. That is His heart. But if the door of the heart is shut, He cannot get in. (See Revelation 3:20.) Only those whose door to their heart is open will receive help, "Blessed are those who mourn, for they shall be comforted" (Matt. 5:4).

Seeing Spiritual Flows From the Negative Side

Sometimes it is easier to see spiritual flows from a negative perspective. Negative flows tend to be more exaggerated and out of balance. Thus, they are easier to spot. Seven basic negative flows that parallel the positive flows given in the Sermon on the Mount are spiritual pride, fear and unbelief, rebellion, lust, bitterness, a critical spirit, and selfish ambition.

It is not hard to visualize someone flowing in bitterness. We can pick up on a critical spirit rather easily. When lust overtakes a person, it soon becomes obvious. When these flows are in the beginning stages, they are hidden, but as they develop over time, words or actions are often not needed to detect a spiritual flow. Over time, these spiritual substances actually begin to show up on peoples' faces. A bitter person has a tightness about him that does not even need words. In the same way, lust, rebellion, and selfish ambition have a look about them that is identifiable.

So how does this help us make sense of life? In the natural realm, there are no guaranteed outcomes. It rains on the just and it rains on the unjust. But in the spiritual realm, the outcomes are much more instantaneous and much more guaranteed. The very first beatitude that mentions "poor in spirit" gives a guaranteed outcome of "theirs is the kingdom of heaven"—present tense. It describes an immediate, guaranteed outcome. When the flow of a person's heart can be described as being "poor in spirit," the Scriptures guarantee that that person has immediate access to the kingdom of God.

For Mary, this concept was the spark of hope that she needed. She had given up hope of truly connecting with God and she firmly believed that she would never be able to have any significant trust with another human being. Over time, Mary was able to learn that the flow of her own heart was setting up the responses coming back to her. Once the negative flow of her heart was identified and changed, over time the responses coming back to her changed.

The Heart: the Key to Understanding Life

When we see the heart, we begin to understand what God is doing and how He is responding. When we see what God is up to, we begin to understand life. If a person embraces bitterness, there is an immediate distancing of his relationship with God and with people. There is no delay. There is no waiting for fruit to show up. Granted, some people don't notice the bitterness and continue to respond to the person as if nothing had changed. Man does tend to look on the outward appearance.

Too often, we are not sensitive to the more intimate levels of connectedness that a spirit-to-spirit connection brings. Instead, we operate at a very practical, workplace level of functional communication. Thus, when we encounter a person who is bitter, we don't even notice that bitterness until it begins to interfere with our ability to function. If we were more sensitive to the heart, we could tell almost instantly when a person becomes bitter and that the intimacy aspect of the communication shuts down. We are now dealing with an outward shell. We are now dealing with mere words and actions. In the workplace that might be acceptable, but in ministry that is the sound of death.

Spiritual life is about being connected to God and others.

The spiritual realm is about relationship. God said that in the day that Adam sinned, he would die. (See Genesis 2:17.) Is the Word of God wrong, or did Adam die on the day that he sinned? He died—not physically, but spiritually. To die spiritually is to be separated from God's Spirit. To be spiritually alive is to be connected to God and others. We think of death as that point at which life ceases to exist, but physical death happens when the spirit separates from the body, not when the spirit ceases to exist. Our spirits are eternal. They never ceases to exist! The Greek word for death, *thanatos* actually means, "to be separated."[1] Biblically, separation equals death.

The person who becomes bitter shuts down any intimacy flow, and shuts the door to potential help. That person is in the process of dying spiritually! The good news is that we have many doors to our hearts. Like a fiber optic phone line, our hearts are capable of multiple connections at any one time. We may be bitter toward one person, but still have open doors of relationship with others. If that were not so, a single root of bitterness would kill us spiritually and there would be no hope for any person to receive help from others.

Heart flows immediately determine what is happening in the spiritual realm, but more gradually impact the natural realm. Things in the natural realm are much more delayed, scattered, and less predictable. A person flowing in bitterness is immediately impacted in the spiritual realm, but it may take a period of time before his relationships begin to deteriorate to the level of his bitterness. That person is able to cover his bitterness with functional communication for a season. In the same way, once a person chooses to forgive, it can take time for others to begin to trust him and relate to him as if he weren't bitter.

Hopefully, you are beginning to get the point. The results of our natural lives can be delayed, scattered, and imperfect, even for those who are trying to walk with God. In the spiritual realm, this is not so. Results are guaranteed.

The Mercy of God's Hammer

Mary began to recognize the power of her own critical spirit. What Mary was giving out would all but guarantee what would come back to her. God's response to a critical spirit is very harsh and confrontational. We see this confrontational response demonstrated by Jesus toward the Pharisees, who also are giving out a critical spirit flow. (See Matthew 23:1–36.) Jesus cut them no slack. Mary had a critical spirit. God confronted her and allowed her to be confronted on a consistent basis.

As human beings, we are made in the image of God. (See Genesis 1:26.) When it comes to spiritual flows, we have instinctive reactions that will mimic God's reaction to those flows. In Mary's life, her critical spirit flowing forth meant that people would be harsh and confrontational back to her. As human beings, our responses to spiritual flows are predictable. To the bitter, we close down and back off. To the rebel, we respond with either fight or flight. With the proud, we are guarded. These human reactions to different spiritual flows are almost automatic!

It was the constant bombardment of harsh confrontation that finally broke Mary down and caused her to seek help. God knows that the only thing that will cause a critical spirit to finally turn and seek Him is to let it be hammered over time. It is not spiteful that God confronts a critical spirit. Confrontation is the only hope a critical spirit has of changing course. Jesus' confrontation of the Pharisees was an act of love.

Mary finally began to see that if she could connect with God and start walking with God, life could change. By simply recognizing her critical spirit, humbling herself, and asking for help, she could connect. Once connected, a softer, more gentle side began to emerge. It was not of her doing; indeed, she had tried for years to be gentler and had failed. The Bible tells us that if we give out judgment, it will return upon our own heads. (See Matthew 7:1–2.) The church had judged her even as she had judged them. There was a face-off and no one was winning. Once she realized God's hand in the face-off, she humbled herself and began to connect with life.

God's Guarantees!

The Sermon on the Mount contains a wonderful list of guarantees. In these verses in Matthew 5:3–9, the first statement is the condition of the heart and the second is the associated promise:

> Blessed are the poor in spirit,
> For theirs is the kingdom of heaven.
> Blessed are those who mourn,
> For they shall be comforted.
> Blessed are the meek,
> For they shall inherit the earth.
> Blessed are those who hunger and thirst for righteousness,

For they shall be filled.
Blessed are the merciful,
For they shall obtain mercy.
Blessed are the pure in heart,
For they shall see God.
Blessed are the peacemakers,
For they shall be called sons of God.

The poor in spirit will be able to access kingdom help. Those who mourn will be comforted. The meek will be able to walk in spiritual authority. Those who hunger and thirst for righteousness will have satisfaction. Those who are merciful will obtain mercy. Those who are pure in heart will see God and understand His ways. Those who are peacemakers will feel the nurturing love that comes from being a child of God.

The flows of the heart always determine the outcomes in life. If there is a consistent outcome in a person's life, all a minister will have to do is trace backward and find the spiritual flow. Someone who has a deep and abiding sense of satisfaction has been hungering and thirsting after doing right. Someone who is feeling comforted has been able to face his pain, mourn properly, and get to a point of healing. The spirit realm is predictable. The natural realm is not.

As a society, we have tried to say that these spiritual flows are just thoughts or emotions, or maybe behavioral patterns. While a bitter person will have bitter thoughts and feelings associated with his bitterness, the bitterness is actually much deeper than thoughts and feelings. It is, as I describe it, a spiritual substance that flows through the vessels of our spiritual heart.

Many who have come to Christ have experienced the deeper nature of these spiritual substances. A person who is bitter has a stirring in his heart to repent. He comes to an altar with God, and receives His love and His life. When he leaves the altar, there is frequently a change not just of spiritual flow (releasing of the bitterness), but of thoughts and feelings. The whole world changes. When we change our spiritual flow, it impacts our thoughts and our feelings at the same time. That happens because the flows of the heart are much deeper and much more substantial.

On the other hand, a person can be told over and over again that bitter thoughts and feelings are wrong. He can examine those thoughts and feelings and realize that they are wrong and even destructive to him as a person. But will that understanding change anything? For Mary, nothing changed when being told how to live. In fact, most of the time a person will continue to walk in his bitterness or critical spirit despite the new knowledge that he should not. There is something deeper, more effective and powerfully healing in ministry when we learn to touch the spirit realm, not just the thoughts and feelings.

"I tried that once!"

Like Mary, too many people are walking around feeling as if God is not capable of helping them with their problems. They have tried the "Jesus thing" and it didn't work. They conclude that God must not love them, or must not want to help them, or maybe is not even able to help them. They think this way because they have had an encounter with the church that did not acquaint them with a true walk in the Spirit. When we walk with God, there are guaranteed outcomes in the spirit, and eventually, even the natural begins to line up with the spiritual flow.

Believers who do not recognize what I am talking about most likely are walking around with negative flows like lust or a critical spirit. They wonder why they are confused and not satisfied! God is simply being faithful to His character and His Word. The one who hungers and thirsts after righteousness is guaranteed satisfaction. The one who lusts will never be satisfied. The one who is pure in heart will see God. The one who is critical will be continually confused and confounded.

It is not just about naming the name of Christ, but about walking with God through Christ. Those who walk with God through Christ will know His fruit. Those who do not walk with God through Christ will not bear His fruit. At best, they will know a human level of fruit that imitates the fruit of God. There is a human level of peace that mimics God's peace, but it falls far short of the glory of God. It falls short of what is available to us if we walk with God through Christ.

Much of the church of today has settled for trying to live for God. We read our Bible. We pray. We attend church. We tithe. And we hope all of this is good enough. God wants us to humble our hearts, reach out to Him, and let His Spirit flow through us. That is the life-style of bearing fruit. Such a life will have great power and authority, and even greater results. It will measure up to the glory of God. But instead of a fruit-bearing life, we settle for a few good works.

True Connection

Connecting with God is simple. First of all, we must recognize when we are not connected. When we are in lust, we are shutting a door to God. When we are in fear, we are shutting another door. It is the same with pride, rebellion, bitterness, a critical spirit, and selfish ambition. Connecting with God is as simple as saying, "God, I am flowing with the wrong spirit. I have embraced bitterness (etc.). I am actually being energized by Satan instead of by You. Please forgive me, God. Help me to return to my created purpose of being a temple for Your presence. I repent of my bitterness toward (_____). I ask You to come and fill me with Your presence. God, please come and bear Your fruit in me, amen."

Mary prayed that kind of prayer, and there was a change. No, it wasn't immediate in terms of a life change. The old thought and action patterns were too ingrained for it to be an overnight change. But Mary became determined to connect with God. Her life was like a huge ship that had been steered astray by a wounded and critical spirit. Large ships don't turn quickly or easily. Mary had to be reminded over and over again to reconnect. The years of negative imprinting were still bearing fruit in her thought patterns and in quick verbal comebacks. It was hard for her to change—but Jesus is the Answer!

There were many around her who did not exactly help the process. Instead of encouraging her because of the moments of connection and grace that were flowing through her, all they could see were the negative comebacks. People are like that. They will see through their own lens of having been wounded. They will condemn the person who is just starting to connect with God through Christ, and in many cases be an influence that would cause that person to give up hope and stop connecting. Those around a person who is just starting to connect must be challenged to see through the eyes of faith. They need to realize that years of substance take time to erase and to look for moments of growth, instead of demanding a consistent pattern of victory immediately.

Mary's life was like a huge ship that had been steered by wounding and a critical spirit.

When we realize that sin is not just about the outward actions and words, but about spiritual flow, it is much easier to connect with God and to stay connected with God. As with Mary, old patterns will still jump in here and there, but we need to focus more inward than outward. If we think we have to wait until we kill someone to repent, then we have been in sin a long, long time. We have gone through stages of bitterness, escalating anger, murderous thoughts, ugly words, and hurtful actions—all because we refused to acknowledge the initial spiritual flow. Sometimes it takes a long time for the grotesque fruit to show up in the natural realm.

In the same way, it can take a period of time for a godly connection to consistently show up in words and actions. The person with a goal of having every word and action become Christlike overnight is not being realistic. Yes, God can and does give immediate deliverances to individuals, but I have never seen God deliver every area within an individual on the spot. Because He is training a heart, He always seems to leave an area of struggle that the person has to dedicate to Him, decision by decision. That takes time.

In the Spirit realm, things are much more immediate. We are either walking with God, or we are not. We are experiencing His presence and are in contact with Him, or we are not. There is a very real and immediate flow that is happening in the person that can change in a moment. If we pay attention to these flows, we will understand where the behaviors are coming from. If we notice flows, the words that come out of our mouths will not surprise us.

The Importance of Words and Actions

None of what I have said means that thoughts, words, and actions are not important. Thoughts, words, and actions are important because they reveal what is going on in our hearts. If it is surfacing in our conscious realm, it is because there is at least some measure of it in our hearts. Thus, every subtle thought is a potential place for repentance and a pleading for God's presence to take over again.

Our thoughts, words, and actions are also important in another way. What comes out of our bodies cements a spiritual flow to our hearts. I can play with the spiritual flow of lust in my mind and it can begin to impact my heart. Even at this thought level, the Bible calls it sin and it begins to do damage. (See Matthew 5:27–28.) Even at this thought level, it is beginning to establish the negative aspects of the spiritual flow in my heart. But when I act out that lust, it does damage in the natural and cements that lust to my heart in a much greater way than mere thoughts can. When I act out lust, my heart actually changes more into the character and nature of that lust. Then the next time I am about to act, that same spiritual substance of lust is there lurking in my heart, begging to be accessed again. What comes through our bodies is extremely important. That is why the Bible commands us to flee, to run from fornication. (See 1 Corinthians 6:18.) It will kill us spiritually.

Just about any negative response to a situation a person is facing can be simplified down to one of the seven negative spiritual flows. Sure, there are hundreds of subtle variations to these flows, but these seven pretty well summarize the negative flows of life. And the seven positive flows from the Sermon on the Mount do a good job of summarizing what it would look like if the life of God were flowing in a person. Another similar list of positive spiritual flows is found in Galatians 5:22–23 where Paul mentions the fruit of the spirit.

Spiritual flows have spiritual outcomes as well as natural outcomes. If we can reverse the spiritual flows, we can reverse the outcomes.

We reverse the spiritual flows by helping people see their flows, own those flows, invite the presence of God to be their center, and then teaching them to walk with God. In the same way that negative words and actions cement negative flows to the heart, ultimately it is obedience to God that will cement godly flows to the heart.

Thus, it is good to memorize Scriptures and repeat them out loud in an area of spiritual struggle. Words and actions are important. However, it is much more effective to memorize and quote Scripture once a connection with God has been established. The spoken word and the godly actions become the fruit of a heart connected and not just a human attempt at being good.

Fighting Upstream

Too many people are trying to do good without addressing the negative substance still residing in their hearts. They serve God out of fear. The fear motivates them to do good works, but the fear guarantees that those works are done with human effort, not with a connectedness to God. In the end, that person will tire and become hard of heart, living a life of ritual and works righteousness. The person who does the same works out of a connectedness to God, will develop a heart of compassion for God and man. Connectedness is life—disconnectedness is death.

We have all heard it said that "Jesus is the Answer." I once saw that as the kind of blanket statement that is a bit naïve. I mused that practical things need practical answers. And how is Jesus the answer for that? The more I have learned about spiritual flows, the more I've come to understand that "Jesus *is* the Answer." Period.

We are either connected to God and flowing with Him and bearing good fruit, or we are not. We are either having a heart that is being nurtured into the image of Christ, or we have a heart that is gradually hardening. Ultimately, all of life's issues point back to the heart and to whether or not we are connected to God.

Adam died spiritually on the day that he disconnected from God. God gave Adam a second chance by seeking him out and offering the skin of an animal as a kind of covering for his sin. No animal can pay the price for sin. This sacrifice, like all sacrifices in the Old Testament, looked forward to the sacrifice Christ would make on the cross. When the Son of God died, He paid the penalty for sin for us so that we could have fellowship restored with God.

The irony is that so few people actually take any significant advantage of the fellowship Christ offers to us through His death. Most try to live a good life, doing the best they can in their own strength. When a crisis comes, they pray. Some send a kind of running mental dialogue toward God. For most people that I know, their walk with God is more accurately described as a man putting forth an effort toward God rather than a real connecting with God grounded in humble, thankful obedience.

Unless we connect with God, we don't have His life. Yes, there are levels of connectedness, and salvation is not dependent on having all the connections of our lives in place with Him. But if we want to be a lifegiver and live a life that bears fruit in Him, we need to be connected to Him. To connect with Him, we need to learn to recognize the flows of our heart that keep us disconnected from Him.

Those who connect with God and walk with Him will never die. Not spiritually, anyway. Though a Christian, Mary was all but dead spiritually. Life was confusing, hopeless, and full of darkness. She had tried to live the Christian life and it had done very little for her. When we try in our own effort to live for God, a sense of futility will be the outcome. When we learn to connect with God and to let Him live through us, we get a very different outcome.

Mary began to truly live spiritually when she began to connect with God. No, I'm not saying that she was not saved before, but I am saying that she was producing much more of the fruit of spiritual death than she was of spiritual life. She had a very limited level of connection. To more fully connect, she had to recognize her heart flows, humble herself, and ask for God's help.

Do you want to make sense of life? Start looking at heart flows. Heart flows produce the harvests of our lives. Heart flows give us the best explanation for some of the outcomes we are getting in life. For Mary, getting away from a focus on words and actions, and turning toward a focus on heart flows, were the changes that brought life. If

God looks first and foremost at the heart, so should we. It is the key to life, to ministry, and to becoming a lifegiver.

> *Father God, I thank You that You have created my heart to flow with Your life. Help me to guard my heart that I might bless You and others! Amen. (Prayer based on Proverbs 4:23.)*

Study Guide

1. What are some of the different ways that a bitter person might respond outwardly? How could a seemingly sweet response still carry a bitter spiritual flow?

2. Define in your own words what is meant in the beatitudes by the phrases "blessed are the poor in spirit" and "blessed are those who mourn." What makes these two things a positive spiritual flow in God's eyes?

3. Why is it often easier to recognize spiritual flows from the negative side than from the positive? Looking through the flows listed, what negative flows do you struggle with? When and how do you struggle?

4. Spiritual flows produce guaranteed outcomes. List some outcomes for both positive and negative flows.

5. Because of her critical flow, Mary and the church had been at odds. How was that face-off resolved? How does this demonstrate the difference between living strengthened by the grace of God versus living in human effort?

6. In a model that focuses on spiritual transformation, what are the roles of thoughts, words, and actions? How do I treat thoughts, words, and actions differently in this model than I would in the prevailing worldview of our culture?

7. According to this chapter, how does Jesus truly become the answer for any and every problem situation? How can you better apply this concept to your life?

Chapter 5

TWO TARGETS

I had just been to a Christian conference—you know, one of those where you get all of the answers and come home ready to save the world. I was younger, and a bit naïve. As soon as I found out that a relative had high blood pressure, I was quick to share with her what I had learned, that bitterness can cause high blood pressure.

I really was somewhat innocent in my comment, but I touched a sore spot and I got a blistering lecture from this woman on how she was not holding bitterness. She had forgiven Linda, and that was that! I had no business suggesting that she was still bitter!

Never mind that I knew nothing about the situation with Linda, but I did know something of this relative's lifestyle. It was not uncommon for her to be railing about someone. My comments were meant to be helpful, general truth. Instead, she admitted her guilt with her tirade. I do believe that in her own mind, she had already pronounced herself innocent. She had done some kind of mental and perhaps verbal admission of forgiveness, but in her heart, she was clearly guilty of holding onto bitterness.

This story illustrates that there are two targets for true, life-changing ministry and not just one. The first target is in the area of our conscious awareness. Most people have some awareness of their current snapshot, their current spiritual presence, and whether or not it needs to be changed. But the deeper and more abiding flows of the heart must also be changed. My relative had a deeply etched flow of bitterness written on her heart. This abiding bitterness could not be overwritten by a simple declaration of innocence.

My relative had short-circuited the forgiveness process by monitoring her thought life. When negative thoughts would come, she would "take them captive." (See 2 Corinthians 10:4–6.) She would declare them to be not true and not a part of her person. In her case, neither her spiritual presence nor her spiritual substance ever changed. What she though to be a current snapshot of forgiveness was nothing but a hypocritical game of self-deception.

Mentally thinking through forgiveness is good (if it is honestly done!), but we must aim for the deeper target of transforming the heart. Mind games don't change the heart. A temporary outward obedience doesn't get the job done. Even the person touched by an experience with God's presence is not necessarily changed. A person is only transformed when he embraces the will of God in body, soul, and spirit, and has been empowered by the Holy Spirit to do so on a consistent basis. It takes the commitment of the total person to reshape the deeper target of a person's spiritual substance.

A person is only transformed when he embraces the will of God in body, soul, and spirit over a period of time.

Spiritual choices are spiritual choices, not necessarily made at a conscious level. It is very common for the son of an alcoholic parent to try to avoid the behavior patterns of an offending parent. Peter was very careful not to follow in the footsteps of his father. His father was abusive and belittling. Peter was quiet and withdrawn. His father burned the family income on alcohol. Peter was careful that not one penny was wasted—on anything. The irony is that Peter's children were just as distant from him as he was from his father. He could not understand it. Why? He was not like his father. Why would his children have nothing to do with him?

Spiritual substance is spiritual substance, regardless of what kind of mental gymnastics of self-defense the mind is able to accomplish. For the father, the mode of operation was outward. Peter turned it inward, but both of them lived in bitterness. The father was selfish and spent his income on himself. The son was selfish and kept it for himself, never "wasting" a penny. Selfishness and bitterness alienate children. The outward behaviors of the two men were different. But the spiritual substance of the two was the same. Peter was able to look at outward actions and pat himself on the back at how he was not like his father. Peter was wrong.

When a person connects with bitterness and stirs its presence into his current flow, he eventually will download it to his recorder. Peter did that. His mind did a great job of rationalizing that he was not bitter. How easy it is to believe a lie! However, as the years went on, the slightest provocation sent him into depression and retreat. He may not have followed the actions of his father, but the poor spiritual health of his life was evidence that something was wrong.

Even with clear evidence in full view that we have bitterness or hatefulness or some other negative substance, we generally find a way to think well of ourselves unless we are a self-hater. In cases of self-hatred, the pattern is to beat others to the punch by punishing self. This too is a form of self-protectionism. It is simply a defense mechanism, but it is a defense mechanism that is intellectually dishonesty. Spiritual presence and spiritual substance don't lie.

As intercessors, we can bring life to a person, even seeing him walk in incredible freedom for a time. Yet this still is not the complete battle. Long-term change comes when a person embraces a consistent flow of spiritual presence leading to a consistent spiritual substance.

Some test the waters of a new spiritual substance only for a season. After an initial trial period, many will reject the new flow simply because it doesn't line up with their childhood choices of spiritual flow. If a person does reject the new flow, the more fleeting nature of current spiritual presence passes and the person returns to the programming of his hard drive. His childhood flow of spiritual presence is reestablished.

Understanding what it takes to rewrite our spiritual substance programming helps us see what a struggle it can be to change. Those who have a significant programming of godly substance written into them don't know how blessed they are. It is these people who will be able to "just change." Those who are able to "just change" look at others with disdain and wonder why they too can't "just change." If a change in behavior doesn't require a significant change in spiritual substance, it will be relatively easy to make. When a substance change is needed, it will take hard work over an extended period of time to be accomplished.

The Role of the Conscience

One of the greatest insights I ever received was when I realized that the conscience of a person is not necessarily reliable. Our conscience is actually a general feeling of the heart of either comfort or discomfort in any situation. In 1 Timothy 4:2, Paul talks about the ability for a person's conscience to be "seared." A person with a seared conscience is no longer able to discern the spiritual feel of a situation. Ironically, these people who have a deadened conscience turn to rules and regulations to try to be good. They still have some knowledge that they are created to be a positive influence, but rules are the best they can do.

This person will feel like he is doing wrong when he is actually doing right.

To put it plainly, there are times we feel guilty when we shouldn't. There are times we feel no guilt when we should. In 1 John 3:20, John tells us that our hearts sometimes condemn us, but that "God is greater than our heart." The consistent scriptural picture is that our conscience is not reliable unless it is being renewed by the current and active influence of the Holy Spirit. If left to ourselves, our consciences will give us a feeling of comfort when we are living in and around something that is spiritually familiar. If bitterness is the norm, we will actually feel somewhat comfortable living around bitterness, despite the fact that bitterness often brings a sharp and painful response from others.

Our conscience was designed to help keep the righteous person righteous. It actually tends to resist change because it is merely a barometer reading that measures against what is recorded in our spiritual substance. This does help keep the righteous person walking in righteousness, because his barometer will say that sin is sin. But it does create a struggle for the person who has ungodly programming. This person will feel like he is doing wrong when he is actually doing right. His spiritual gauge has been turned up side down by the wrong programming.

One couple that I counseled had frequent screaming matches with one another and often let the screaming escalate to some sort of physical violence. Both had come from turbulent homes. This was their spiritual norm. With dutiful obedience, they agreed not to speak a harsh word or to act out any physical violence for a week. Guess what they said at the end of that week? "Pastor, we did what you said. We actually made it through the whole week without screaming or fighting. But it was one of the most uncomfortable weeks of our entire lives."

What these two were telling me is what I am trying to share with you—our conscience, our general comfort level, comes out of our spiritual past. Change is very difficult for the conscience, and typically only happens when life is too painful to go on without change. We don't want to change. It brings the unfamiliar to our lives. It doesn't feel right. It is uncomfortable.

Certainly, the person who is able to connect with the presence of God will have God's help to renew and transform the conscience. But even then it is a fight. Our inner substance, written down from past experiences, does tend to dominate our current choice of programming. We are more comfortable with what is familiar.

A bitter person connects with bitter thoughts and then bitter people, which results in a continual flow of bitter presence. That flow of bitter presence reinforces the bitter substance within. The conscience is at "peace." That is why a person can be in the middle of an adulterous situation and say that he is "at peace" with himself. He thinks that his peace means that he is OK. But in reality, it is an explicit indictment of how far his conscience has fallen from the standard of God.

If it doesn't line up with God's Word, it is not O.K.

If it doesn't line up with God's Word, it is not OK. It doesn't matter how much peace there is in a person's conscience, the Word of God must be preeminent. It has to be that way because our consciences are simply a general guide. Our consciences are only good to the extent that we are connected to God and flowing with God, or to the extent that we have a godly foundation from our past.

People with a terribly sinful heritage can still connect with God. They do feel the tug of His pull on their consciences. God does intervene in the affairs of men. But apart from that pull, there is little or no hope for those who do not have the things of God written into their basic programming. The conscience will always pull the ungodly back into the darkness. (See John 3:19.) The darkness in the unrighteous will then make it difficult to connect with God or with others.

We tend to like what is familiar. We connect with what we know. To do otherwise is to set up a war within and it usually doesn't "feel right." The spiritual feeler of a person can actually cause that person to block out God and the godly. It sounds crazy, but it is true.

Spiritual Substance Determines Our Connections

We generally don't realize that our current spiritual presence, coming out of our spiritual substance, is what determines our spiritual connections. In plain language, we will likely choose to connect with what we are. Bitterness chooses bitterness. Pride chooses pride. Compassion chooses compassion. The person who goes to his spiritual memory bank and accesses a God-derived peace will actually be inviting the presence of God to come alongside and strengthen that peace.

The person who instead chooses a more self-reliant spiritual flow will not be able to connect with God. Because of our tendency toward self-deception, he will instead access a human level of peace. This peace could best be described as an absence from immediate trouble, or perhaps there is enough spiritual pride also present to reassure the person that he has everything under control. This is not a peace that comes from connectedness to God, but it looks enough like the real thing to often fool people into thinking that their spiritual flows are lining up with God.

Whatever is flowing in our current spiritual presence will also determine our level of connectedness with people. Distrust will refuse almost all levels of connectedness. In cases of severe distrust, all interaction happens through the soulish realm—the mind, the will, and the emotions. There is no sense of spiritual connection and because we are spiritual beings, the relationship will seem hollow. Real change toward godliness is not possible unless there is a spiritual connection with godly people or with God Himself.

A person flowing in unforgiveness can only connect spiritually with another person willing to receive an offense. As a pastor, I have witnessed this multiple times. All it takes is a little spiritual pride and two people begin to butt heads. Pride naturally brings division. For a season, they are enemies—until one of them is able to pass off a little gossip to the next, activating an offense toward a third person in the process. Suddenly, because of a common enemy, the pride that had been a divide is eclipsed by a new spiritual flow: bitterness. These two persons of like substance connect and there is a sense of intimacy— for a time.

Two people walking in unforgiveness can never have any significant, on-going intimacy. The fruit of negative spiritual substance produces disconnectedness, which is the essence of spiritual death. Have you ever wondered why mortal enemies become instant friends if they can only galvanize against a common enemy? Hitler used this technique of developing a common enemy to create a semblance of unity. It worked for a season. Through hyping a common enemy, darkness can experience a type of intimacy. Though this artificial "connectedness" is an illusion, people will play the game with each other because the illusion of being connected feels better than having no intimacy at all.

Rewritten in the Image of Christ

The ultimate goal of the lifegiver is to see the spiritual storehouse of another person completely overwritten by the very image and presence of God. A change in behavior is good, but it may not be indicative of a total victory. It might just be another version of bad substance. Smokers often simply change one addiction for another. They change from smoking to overeating or drinking or some other self-indulgence. There is a behavior change, but not a substance change.

To have a godly presence for a few moments is good, but it is fleeting and will not give permanent victory. Our goal must be to point the person toward a complete rewrite of his inner man into the image of Christ. This takes time and it cannot be done without the cooperation of the person, without his saying "Amen" to the recording of new imprints upon his heart.

There are those who would protest what I am saying, who would describe being born again as some kind of complete download that changes everything instantaneously. I don't think the Scriptures support that kind of view. Hebrews 6:4–6 describes the process: "For it is impossible for those who were once enlightened, and have tasted the heavenly gift, and have become partakers of the Holy Spirit, and have tasted the good word of God and the powers of the age to come, if they fall away, to renew them again to repentance, since they crucify again for themselves the Son of God, and put Him to an open shame."

Most people focus on the last part of these verses, the falling away, and then fight over whether or not the person who fell away was "saved" or not. I think that misses the incredible description that we have of an interaction with God. The interaction is described in three ways: being enlightened, having tasted of the heavenly gift, and having become partakers of the Holy Spirit. This language fits very well into the model that I have presented. Whether saved or not, the person's radio temporarily comes upon the God station and tastes of the heavenly gift. There is a temporary enlightening, a temporary partaking of the Holy Spirit.

Mixed Substance

Even the ungodly can temporarily connect with God because none of us is completely full of one kind of substance. We are all a mixture of both the godly and the ungodly. Even the most ungodly person can temporarily tune in to the station of God's presence by allowing the good within him to be temporarily accessed. He can taste of God's presence, experience it, and still not choose to download its imprint into his heart.

The ungodly refuse to trust God, remaining in control of the radio station and the "Save" button and remain unsaved. In doing so, they are crucifying Christ all over again. Their current choice is the spiritual equivalent of the choice of those who put Christ to death. The godly recognize the foolishness of being in control of the radio station and surrender the overall control to God. They choose to trust Christ. They embrace His imprints and the change process begins. Situation by situation, the saved are presented with new choices of staying connected with God or rejecting His current presence. Though some temporarily may turn away, hopefully the overall decision of trusting Christ is sealed and settled.

Instantaneous or Progressive?

For the better part of two thousand years, the church has fought over whether or not sanctification (the process of changing from being ungodly to being godly) is instantaneous or progressive. Does it happen all at once as a gift from God, or is it put in place one decision at a time? The answer is "Yes." Spiritual presence is more or less instantaneous. We connect with it. We receive it. And we are instantly changed by it. We get a sense of God's forgiveness and His love instantly begins to flow through us. But then something happens and that deeper, more abiding part of us called spiritual substance gets triggered and we are angry all over again. What happened? Have we not changed?

Spiritual substance is solid and eternal, and it must be overwritten one choice at a time. In Hebrews 10:14 it says, "For by one offering

He has perfected forever those who are being sanctified." Notice the tenses of the verbs in this verse. The death of Christ on the cross has "perfected forever" those who come to Him. It is done. When we approach Him it is already completed and can be given as a gift instantly. But the second part of the verse refers to those who "are being sanctified." Those who have already received sanctification as a gift must continually appropriate that gift into their person through daily choices.

In ministering to others, we don't have one target. We have two. Impacting a person's spiritual presence is not enough. There may be an immediate change by inviting God in, but the work has only begun. We need to continue to nurture them until we see a substantive transformation. There can be a tasting and testing that goes on for a season with little or no permanent transformation. We must continue to intercede until the character and nature of the person is transformed. This long-term change cannot happen apart from the instantaneous but on-going gift of the Spirit of God and His presence. It is instantaneous. And it is progressive.

Too often, we stop short of victory and then we wonder what went wrong. We pray the Jimmy's of the world through to a point of godly presence and we think our job is done. It is not. There are two targets and one is much more difficult to change, but once it has changed, it is also much more resistant to falling away from God than the other.

Godly character and godly substance are solid. They will continue to bear good fruit for years to come; yes, even for generations to come. Substance is passed from person to person, even in the very young child, ultimately shaping nations in ways we cannot even imagine. The faith of Abraham was a godly foundation for millions who followed him. Who knows how many people we touch when we lay a godly foundation in one human heart! It is solid. It is lasting. It is, in fact, eternal. When we shape a heart, we shape a future.

My Lord and my God, I give You permission to try the reins of my heart. Test what is in me and expose that which is not of You and change it. I want to be fully Yours inside and out. I don't want to come to Judgment Day thinking that I have been serving You when I haven't been. God, test me and cleanse my heart. Amen. (Prayer based on Jeremiah 17:9–10; Psalm 139:23–24.)

Study Guide

1. Describe spiritual presence and spiritual substance in your own words.

2. How can the mind be thinking one thing and the spiritual reality be completely different from how the mind perceives it? Are there instances in your life where you have seen this to be true?

3. How were Peter and his father the same? How were they different?

4. Explain when the conscience is reliable and when it is not. How do we know when our conscience is reliable? What is the ultimate test for all issues of conscience?

5. How do we move from the Hebrews 6 process of testing and tasting of the things of God to a more permanent recording of His substance into our person?

6. How does this presence/substance theology answer an age-old theological question?

7. In both spiritual presence and spiritual substance, what are your greatest areas of battle?

Chapter 6

THE IMPOSTORS

I actually feel closest to God after I've had a few beers."

Well, that certainly got my attention, to say the least. Coming from a tradition that is not really open to any alcoholic consumption, I was not feeling too positive toward what I was hearing from Bill. Even if I was from a tradition that was accepting of alcohol, I don't think I would feel good about needing a drug-induced state to feel closer to God. It just doesn't quite wash with true spirituality.

So how did I respond to that person? Actually, it was not the first time that I had heard something like that. As long as I give people the freedom to be open and honest, it is not likely to be the last. In fact, it even makes perfect sense in a spiritual substance model. Do you think I am losing it this time? Maybe. But then, perhaps we can learn a few things.

I got a huge breakthrough in my ability to work with people when I started seeing a cycle that we all go through in our pursuit of God or in our attempt to be a good person. Nobody wants to be a failure. We all want to prove ourselves. Because of this desire, the first stop in the cycle is a Herculean human effort to get it right. We do our best to be our best until we finally have no energy left and then we hit a burnout phase. After a few trips into burnout, most will then slide into an, "I don't care what I do any more" phase. This is where the bad behavior surfaces. The last two phases of the cycle are a time of humility and finally a time of connecting with God. This "life cycle" is very predictable in most people. It looks like this:

The Life Cycle

Man in the Image of God
Connected and Empowered

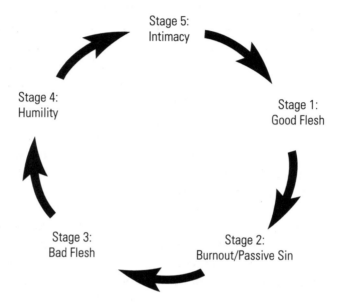

Stage 5:
Intimacy

Stage 4:
Humility

Stage 1:
Good Flesh

Stage 3:
Bad Flesh

Stage 2:
Burnout/Passive Sin

Selfish and Isolated
The Image of Man Without God

Good Flesh

When the Scriptures talk about our flesh, occasionally they are referring to the physical body. More often, especially in Paul's writings
and especially so in Romans 8, they are referring to that part of us
that has evil tendencies. Believe it or not, it is not just our bodies that
have evil tendencies. Our minds can get started on a bad pattern,
or we can develop a very bad attitude. Yes, our souls and our spirits
participate in any evil right along with our bodies. It is not just the
eyes that crave the porn—it is the heart, too.

Almost every person I know defines something in his or her life as the "flesh"—that is, the bad habits, actions, or words that should not be a part of the normal routine. In today's world, we are defining less and less as "flesh," but it is still human nature to separate the good from the bad. It makes sense to us that there are good behaviors and bad behaviors, and so it would make sense according to the previous paragraph to give bad behaviors the biblical name of *flesh*.

So why do I call the first stage "good flesh"? Isn't that a contradiction of terms? If it is good, it shouldn't be called flesh, and if it is flesh, it should not be described as being good. The answer is that behavior alone does not tell the whole story. Good behavior can have bad motives. We can behave well to manipulate or to gain an advantage. We can use behavior to try to bring glory to ourselves. We can even behave well just because we want to think well of ourselves, which is one of our greatest tendencies!

Good behavior with a wrong heart motive does not measure up to the standard of God. It is still good behavior, so I call it good, but it has a bad element to it. So I call it *flesh*—good flesh. We all try to be loving (which is a good behavior!), but God's standard for love is much higher than the human standard for love. We settle for positive goose bumps. We settle for that emotional feeling that comes when others are making us feel good about self or we are feeling good about others. God asks for patience and forgiveness and humility—but we redefine love, set it at a standard that we think we can meet, and then give it our best shot. We give it our best human effort, but we fall short of what He wants for our lives.

"Our Best Shot"

I believe that every person ultimately knows that "our best shot" is all we are doing. We are created with software from God that lets us know that there is something better that could be achieved. Yet it remains just out of reach. And it starts to get a little frustrating. After a while, we realize that our attempt at being good is nothing more than an impostor, an attempt at imitating the way God wants us to live.

Good flesh is living life solely at a human level. It is a human level of peace. The job is fine. My wife loves me. My car is running right. Human peace. But let one thing to go wrong, and I struggle. The truth is, we were never made to live at a human level. We were made to be continually strengthened by the presence of God. Especially in a fallen world, we cannot measure up to God's standard on our own.

Even if we were not under the influence of Adam's sin nature, we would struggle trying to live the way God wants using only human strength. We are made to be continually energized by God. When living at a human level, we are the Energizer Bunny. We may last for a long time, longer than any other person we know. But the truth is we will still run out of energy sooner or later.

Yet, this is where we tend to go—to the place of good flesh. The Energizer Bunny is on the loose trying to do good. Since the Fall, this has become our natural resting place. It is continually our point of return. Good flesh. Human effort to do good. We stay there as long as we can. "I can do it by myself," we think, and the attitude of the three-year-old reigns in us. We press and we press. Then we drop off a cliff.

Desperately Trying to Keep It Together!

"I could be godly if it weren't for the stupid people that I have to put up with." I've actually had someone give me that line. That is the next step in the good flesh process. We do something stupid, making it obvious that we are falling short of the standard written on our hearts. Yet, instead of giving in to the truth, we generally tend to get brittle. We blame others for our fall. We imagine that if circumstances were just different, we really could live up to the standard. We try to create walls, barriers, or crutches to live by that make it easier for us not to fail. But the harder we try, the more we force controls on life, the more uptight we become spiritually. It is the result of someone fighting the good flesh fight a little too long.

Next come the rules. A person might tell himself, "I will stay away from porn if I can just get the women around me not to dress in such a provocative way. I might even need to go into the ministry in order to create a less provocative atmosphere. I try more and more outward solutions, even good and biblical solutions to try to fix my problem. But all the while, I am missing the real solution. I am refusing to see and own the substance of my own heart. Why? Because I am in the good-flesh zone. My works aren't that bad. I am walking in love, as near as I can tell. Never mind that my wife and my children feel spiritually abused. Never mind that my patience is a little on the thin side. Never mind that I am extremely dependent on rules. Never mind that one minute I am judging others and the next I am down on myself. Never mind that I am playing the good flesh game of the "impostor." These are the result of living life the best I can without the help of God.

We try to create walls, barriers, or crutches to live by that make it easier for us not to fail.

Burnout

The natural man only has so much energy. Without the energizing work of the Holy Spirit, our batteries will run down. We will finally tire of the press and become fully depressed, giving it all up. For a few moments (or in some cases for weeks or years), it all comes crashing down and we live in a hopeless state. This is the second stage of the cycle and it almost always follows our first and primary stage of good flesh.

For some, the time of burnout is a time of sleeping. There is a shut down from life, waiting for the natural energy to return so that they can return to their natural state—good flesh. The depressive time is not fun. It is not productive. It does not feel good to us as human beings. There is no meaning there, though some learn to find meaning in self-pity. By wallowing in the sense of having been treated extremely bad, there is a kind of martyr complex that can develop. That feels kind of good to the ego. It gives some meaning to this depressive hole, and this lures some to continue to live in this state. For most, even that gets old after a while. When there is enough energy, the person usually will return to stage one to start the cycle all over again. If not, stage three is about to enter the picture.

Bad Flesh

What is stage three? "If you can't beat them, join them!" Or, "If you can't be good, you might as well enjoy being bad. So go for it with all the gusto you can muster." Sooner or later, when success in the good flesh stage falls through, the ego can't take it any more. It is time to throw away the standards and enjoy life. "If I'm going to do wrong anyway, I might as well do wrong with a vengeance!" That is the cry of stage three, which I call our *bad flesh.* In some ways, it is an adjustment needed for survival. The depression of burnout is total death. After being in a depressed state, bad flesh feels like life for the first time in a long time. How can it be wrong?

Coming out of stage two, a person's judgment is warped. Dead hopelessness warps any sense of conscience and stirs the "I deserve better" part of the heart. Evil doesn't seem like evil any more. It is fun, alive; so much better than the good flesh stage where life is nothing but striving and failing. Here, there is no failure. There are no rules. If there are no rules, if there are no standards, there can be no failure. It is every man for himself. Grab all you can get. That is the rule and it is fun.

In addition, the ego in stage three draws comparisons between its current stage three romp and the depressive weight of stage two. There is no comparison. This stage is life. Yes, there is no doubt. This is the best of the three. The mind is in full-scale rationalization. Conscience is gone. Partying is in. And it all seems to make sense. Why would anyone prefer stage one? No one could prefer stage two. This must be all life has to offer. The restraints come off, and life is good.

Then the fruit of a stage three lifestyle kicks in. It's called the morning after. What a man sows, that he shall reap (Gal. 6:8). Suddenly life is not so good. Pain returns like a crashing tidal wave, with its secondary and tertiary shocks. Reality has come home and life is not so good. At this point, the rationalizing comes to a halt, the reality side of the thought life kicks back in with a bit of conscience returning, and the good flesh effort takes center stage.

Three Stages, Same Flesh

People play in stages one, two, and three over and over again. They are not always in order. They can jump from one to another, because they are all descriptions of flesh. We just don't see them that way. One is good flesh. One is depressive flesh. One is actively bad flesh. But they are all flesh.

Most people actually move from some form of active flesh (whether good or bad) to passive flesh. The person who has spiritual pride is likely to start in the stage one good flesh area. He will set out to prove that he is the best. He will read more Scriptures, witness to more people, and lay his life down more times than anyone he knows. All of this he will do in the name of pride. It might be good works, but it is still flesh. It is the wrong motivation.

After a while, this person will begin to burn out and slide into stage two. He will begin to dwell on the fact that nobody is noticing his work. He is not getting the level of appreciation that he thinks he ought to get. It just isn't fair. He begins to pull back. He is beginning to move into the passive. It is still spiritual pride. It is still an "I deserve better" mode, which is pride. But now it is moving from an active, trying to prove self to others, to a passive, smoldering self-pity state. Stage one is active pride. Stage two is passive pride.

I describe this charade as the flip side of the same coin. One is heads. One is tails. But it is all the same substance.

A person may go through this same charade over and over, not realizing that the ruling spiritual substance has never changed. I describe it as the flip side of the same coin. One is heads. One is tails. One is stage one. One is stage two. We play heads for a while. Then we play tails. But it is the same coin. The depressive behaviors of the burnout stage are usually no different in substance from the good flesh stage.

When a person finally slips out of stages one and two and goes into stage three, most of the time there is no significant change in spiritual substance. If a person has a godly heritage and is surrounded by relatively good circumstances, he may live most of his life in stages one and two with minimal visits to the bad flesh stage. However, when outside pressures finally overtake the inner spiritual strength, his substance will be exposed for what it is in some kind of active display of sin.

Once the pressure of temptation reaches the breaking point, his spiritual pride tinged with self-pity will turn to revenge or perhaps to a spiritual rampage, which will seem easily justified by the Word of God. His substance hasn't changed from stages one and two. It is still spiritual pride. His outward actions have changed and he goes on a rampage. In some cases, the rampage is headlong evil or partying. He parties with "the best" of them. That is pride. In some cases, pride joins with a critical spirit and becomes outwardly vicious. There are as many expressions of sin as there are people. The outward expressions change from stages one to three, but flesh is flesh. Pride is pride. It will look different in each of the stages, but in many ways, they are all the same.

MO's and Stages

I need to take a quick detour to integrate the topic of MO's (modes of operation) with the stages. When a spiritual substance gets triggered, it usually results in an MO, which is simply another name for an outward response that becomes a pattern of behavior. A person with a critical spirit might fall into a pattern of verbal assaults or may instead choose to be quiet but very sullen. As human beings, we are very patterned in our behaviors and we tend to retreat into these patterns to make our days easier to manage.

Most people have an active MO and a passive MO. The active MO is usually some sort of good flesh MO, something that generates some positive results for the person. An insecure person becomes a control freak, but is able to feel good about it because it gives him a sense of being organized and together. That same insecure person will often have a passive MO (stage two) of retreat into self because "nobody likes me" or "the world is against me." Again, it is the same substance coming out in a passive retreat from life. Almost everyone vacillates consistently between an active and a passive MO (stage one and stage two behavior).

In many cases, the person also has a stage three MO that is basically the same substance. The insecure person gets tired of the stage one—stage two dance and moves from "the world hates me" to "I'm going to hate the world first." This person moves from a passive world of self-pity, to an active world of sharp comments and revenge. The primary underlying substance is still insecurity. Little has changed except the outward expression. It's just that the person now feels justified in turning his good flesh MO into an active bad flesh attack.

Three MO's, Same Substance

We all have MO's that serve as a kind of cover for the substance within, but as we change stages it will give the appearance that we have multiple patterns of behavior. In a way we do. We have stage one, stage two, and stage three behavior all being animated by the same substance. When we first look at a person, it may look like the person has no rhyme or reason to his behavior. It may look like he is all over the map. The real situation is likely to be much simpler than you would think at first.

Spiritual substance is spiritual substance. It just changes in appearance. For some people, the illusion of good flesh is enough. They play games, thinking they are fine. For others, stages two or three become familiar playgrounds. Fortunately, there is a stage four and a stage five, but these require a change in substance.

The first three stages are the playground of the impostor, the one who is doing his best to do good, but is doing it in his own strength. God never created us to be good. He created us to be godly. We can only be godly when we are connected to God's energizing presence and renewed in Him. We are created to be a temple of God.

Without God's presence, we are doomed to the life of an impostor. Whether it is stage one-, stage two-, or stage three-behavior makes no difference. It falls short of the glory of God. But praise God, there is something better! Are you ready to move beyond the life of an impostor?

> *God, I thank You that You are not the author of confusion, but of wisdom and life and peace. You give understanding to those who ask and life to those who turn away from self to seek You. God, bring a clarity to my thoughts and help me to better understand how to serve You. Amen. (Prayer based on 1 Corinthians 14:33; James 1:5, 3:16.)*

Study Guide

1. What is the biblical concept of the word *flesh* that is most commonly used?

2. What does this chapter mean by the term *good flesh*? Even though many of its works of this stage are good, why is it still called flesh?

3. List some of the things a person will do to try to keep himself in the good works zone, though these things will begin to make him "brittle." What does the chapter mean by the description *brittle*?

4. Even though stage two is not pleasant at all, what causes people to go there? What pleasure do some find in stage two that gives them some reason to stay there?

5. What causes the loss of conscience that makes stage three possible? What brings the return of conscience?

6. What is an MO? How do different MO's give the illusion that a person is actually manifesting several different problem areas?

7. The three stages are actually three outward forms of the same spiritual flow. What kind of spiritual flow in your life would illustrate this three-stage dance?

Chapter 7

WHY BROKENNESS?

L uke was distraught. He could not figure out why none of his children were serving God. Luke and his wife had been exemplary Christians. They had been in church every time the doors were open. Yet, none of their children were serving God. Why? Luke was a leader in the church. A tither. He had been faithful in every way. It made no sense. Why the dysfunction in his family? Why the hardness of heart? There had been suicide attempts, alcoholism, and generally out-of-control lives. Yet through it all, Luke remained steady. As faithful as Job. Unwavering.

Luke is a poster child for the good flesh lifestyle. For a person to move into the God-connected stages of the cycle, he must allow God to break down his confidence in self. The events of this life need to create a sense of our need for God. For Luke, he remained resolute to the end. He would overcome. His faith in God would win out. The problem is that it was "his" faith in God. Faith is a gift that is received from God when we realize that in and of ourselves we are not adequate to the task. (See Ephesians 2:8.) Instead, Luke continued to press on, believing that the next time would be different. Next time, his faith would prevail. There is a difference between God's faith and our faith. The man living in the good flesh lifestyle never recognizes that difference and never moves into the God-connected stages of the cycle. Before we study the last two stages of the life cycle, we need to fully understand the biblical concept of *brokenness*.

God's Paradoxes

The Bible is full of paradoxes: dying to self so that we might live, Christ becoming sin for us so that we might become righteousness, the Servant of all being the greatest of all. These are a few of the paradoxes. The idea of brokenness is just one more. "Blessed are the poor in spirit, for theirs is the kingdom of heaven" (Matt. 5:3). Why would God want us to be "poor in spirit"? Why would Jesus want us to be in a downtrodden, beat up, and helpless state? Why would He even allow the kind of world where we would have to go through such incredible pain?

Jesus' target of reaching out to the hurting is taken to another level in what is often called Jesus' mission statement:

> The Spirit of the Lord is upon Me, because He has anointed Me to preach the gospel to the poor; He has sent Me to heal the brokenhearted, to proclaim liberty to the captives and recovery of sight to the blind, to set at liberty those who are oppressed; to proclaim the acceptable year of the Lord.
>
> —Luke 4:18–19

Notice the repetition of terms—*poor, brokenhearted, captives, blind, oppressed*. It is all but impossible to miss. This takes "poor in spirit" to another level. It seems like the only ones that Jesus cares about are those in pain. But, why? It appears that these conditions are a prerequisite for being a candidate for the ministry of Christ. Why wouldn't He come to those who are walking in righteousness? Why wouldn't He come to the strong? Why wouldn't He at least choose some who had their act together to minister to the hurting? Do we have to come to a place of complete brokenness before we can receive His ministry?

The pathway to intimacy with God is not one we would have designed or chosen. To get to the final two stages in the cycle, we must go through a time of brokenness. I did not say a time of "being broken," but a time of brokenness. Hopefully, there is a difference, which this chapter will illustrate.

There are many Luke's in this world, who have seasons of being broken, but who never enter into brokenness. Without brokenness, we can never fully connect with God, never fully enter into intimacy with Him. God's ultimate goal for us is intimacy with Him and the transformation of our lives that comes through that intimacy.

God's Mercy

The answer to the question of "Why is brokenness necessary?" is not necessarily found in the heart of God, but more completely in the heart of man. God does have compassion on the Luke's of this world. In fact, God has the same level and kind of compassion toward all men, yet some people seem to activate the flow of the mercy of God and some do not. One clue to understanding why God's compassion flows to some and not others is found in James 4:6, "God resists the proud, but gives grace to the humble." There is something in the heart of God that is repulsed by pride, and drawn to those whose hearts are broken and crying out for help. That is certainly part of the answer as to why we must come through the pathway of brokenness.

However, I believe that the primary answer to the question of "Why brokenness?" lies in the heart of man. Jeremiah 17:9 tells us that, "The heart is deceitful above all things, and desperately wicked; who can know it?" The heart of man is "deceitful" above all things. More than any other tendency, our heart is "deceitful." If our heart is so prone to deceive, who does it try to deceive? Who is being fooled?

Before we answer that, let's look at one more Scripture passage: "All we like sheep have gone astray; we have turned, every one, to his own way; and the LORD has laid on Him the iniquity of us all" (Isa. 53:6). Notice the middle of the verse: "we have turned, everyone, to his own way." This is a second great tendency of the heart. It tends to flow according to what it knows. It will respond according to what is currently stored there. It will go "its own way."

*As long as a man has an ounce of spirit left, as long
as he is having any success with a good flesh effort,
he will man the ship and fight the battle.*

I believe the heart is "deceitful above all things" because it tends to defend itself in all things. It chooses to go its own way. The defense mechanisms of the heart are elaborate and efficient. As long as a man has an ounce of spirit left, as long as he is having any success with a good flesh effort, he will man the ship and fight the battle. Even God is seen as an Intruder if He is asking for a change. After all, the second great tendency of the heart is to go "his own way." Part of going "his own way" is resisting change. Part of going "his own way" is resisting the change agent. The heart prefers to be in control of its own destiny.

It's not that God doesn't want to help those who are on a more even keel. He can't help them. For Him to minister to us, we have to invite His presence. Most of us are far more comfortable with things as they are than we are with the presence of God invading our space. If He comes, we have to give up some of our pettiness. Oh, how we like to defend our pettiness! We like to go our "own way."

Resisting Change

We have a spiritual man with spiritual potential. Over the years, it has established a pattern of spiritual presence, and one of the greatest tendencies of the heart is to resist any change to that pattern of presence. In other words, one of our tendencies is to resist the Spirit of God. His presence brings a change to our presence. It is not our natural inclination to embrace that change.

For the person who is mostly satisfied with His current position in life, this tendency is elevated to fortress status. God would have to come in with a battering ram to get through. For the one who is beat down and broken, the spirit of the man is in pain. The prospect of change is reasonably inviting. He is much more likely to embrace another presence; anything that might bring relief.

No, it is not so much about the heart of God as it is the heart of man. Notice, the verse doesn't say that God comes to those who have been beat up, but to the "poor in spirit." The wise have learned to embrace change, to embrace the Spirit of God without having to be battered. They have become "poor in spirit" by choice. Some who are battered and bruised only become harder. The chip on their shoulder becomes more pronounced and the protection of self is built into an even higher fortress. No poor in spirit there; no welcoming of the soothing presence of God. No, there is only a high fence of bitterness and pride.

It is not to the beat down that God comes, but to the poor in spirit—those who are ready to welcome Him at any cost. The poor in spirit are ready to become His slaves. Some only learn to serve Him by being reduced to slavery; by being humbled by bit and bridle. (See Psalm 32:9.) These slowly learn to walk with God after several trips into stage three, but at the expense of great pain. Others are bondservants who choose to be poor in spirit without having to be humbled at the expense of pain. These are the ones who learn to recognize the good flesh for what it is—a selfish attempt to prove oneself to God without God's help. These will be honored by God and will serve with minimal pain.

Finding Our Wall

For most of us, we need to hit the wall. Most of us never fully embrace the lordship of Christ until we hit bottom—until our confidence in self is utterly bankrupt. As long as there is one ounce of faith in self left, we will choose the self route. We will choose our current state over what is being offered to us by Christ. We will see what we now have as holy, and what is being offered as vile. Are we ever wrong most of the time!

Those who start with a righteous heritage have the hardest time with this one. Their good flesh is actually pretty good. They have much in themselves that is right. They have much to legitimately protect. It is hard for them to choose to become "poor in spirit." It is much easier to coast on a relatively good spiritual substance with seemingly good spiritual fruit, but minimal life. Being a lifegiver is not about being relatively good; it is about being connected with the Holy Spirit. It is His fruit that we are to produce, and not relatively good works. His fruit only comes from the person actively connected to Him. (See John 15:4.) The "relatively righteous" often fail to see the need to stay connected.

Most of us never fully embrace the Lordship of Christ until we hit bottom.

The work of God begins when we see the need for His presence in order to produce His fruit. It begins when we become "poor in spirit." We are prone to resist His presence until we hit a wall. God rewards us according to the amount of His fruit, which is produced through us, and since He loves us, it is His mercy to let us hit the wall. Without the wall, most of us will never produce His fruit. We will never move into the intimacy stages of the cycle. We will merely produce good works. It takes the discipline of God for us to move past self and into Him.

Luke's Story

Luke was a very good man, but in all my contacts with him, I never once detected any sense of the active presence or voice of God. He was a good man, doing good things. He was a leader of the church. But where was the God of today? I deliberately gave him a number of opportunities, thinking that he would surely catch on to the voice of God, but to no avail. In a service where the Spirit was clearly flowing in a given direction, I would give him verbal cues as to what God was doing and then ask him to pray. He would pray a nice, flowing prayer that sounded excellent. But it had little or nothing to do with what God was doing at the moment.

When the Spirit seemed to be directing a time of quiet waiting, Luke would jump to his feet and pray out in a way that shattered the spirit of the moment. At times when there was an obvious prompting for prayer, Luke would be utterly silent. I was continually dumb-founded at this good man's inability to sense the flow of what God was doing and to respond appropriately. What he did was never technically wrong. It simply lacked life. It lacked connection. It lacked the presence and empowering of the Spirit of God.

As time went on, I began to realize that Luke was like a little kid, wanting and needing approval or attention. His religious performances fit that spiritual model. "Look at me!" he seemed to cry with every word or deed. Is that about age five? "Look at me, Daddy! Look at me!"

This one was not a success story. I did not fully understand then some of the principles that I now know. I didn't know enough to probe his childhood, to find out what may have frozen him at age five. Tragically, a frozen spiritual child produced children after his own kind. Oh, he didn't look like a child. He had a Job-level of righteous-ness. Unfortunately, it was a, "Look at me!" type of righteousness. It was not a "connected-to-God fruit-overflowing" righteousness. His fruit did not line up with his works, but it did line up with the fruit of an unconnected heart, a heart of immaturity and selfishness.

Luke had hit one wall after another. He had lost a young child in a tragic accident. His wife lived from sickness to sickness. His children lived from stupidity to calamity. There was enough pain stacked end-to-end to have crushed a typical man. Yet, it all seemed to run off him, leaving little or no trace of having been there. Most of the time, he had a happy-go-lucky countenance, as if nothing of any great pain had ever happened to him.

In the end, I concluded that Luke had created a wall of his own. He had built a fortress around his human feelings, an attempt to protect himself from the intense pain that he could no longer endure. He had created a wall to keep him from hitting the wall. He had created a wall to prevent him from ever reaching the end of himself. He had created a wall to keep him from having to depend on someone or something else. But he was, after all, a very good man—and that goodness was part of his wall.

God's Strength

For a man to come to the end of himself is one of the greatest gifts God can ever give. For when we are weak, that is when He is strong. (See 2 Corinthians 12:9.) One little strand of His strength is so much stronger than our greatest effort could ever be. Oh, how much we need to come to the end of ourselves! And, oh, how we fight anything that would take us there! "Blessed are the poor in spirit, for theirs is the kingdom of heaven" (Matt. 5:3).

Luke had set up a legacy in his children of self-reliance. Like their father, the children would play with religion, but in their lives, only for a time and a season. They were not sold out as he was to a system of works, but much more strongly manifested the "Look at me!" fruit. If they could gain attention through religious effort for a season, that was fine. If they could gain attention through a suicide effort, that too was fine. "Look at me!" seemed to be the strongest of all seeds passed to the next generation. It was a seed that guaranteed that the walls of life would not bring a sense of humility or true repentance, but rather a headlong slide into insanity.

Luke had set up a legacy in his children of self-reliance.

The lives of the children were a race from self-indulgence to excessive goodness and then back to self-indulgence. The pendulum was swinging in the wrong plane. It never seemed to cross paths with humility, true repentance, or a dependence on God. The swinging pendulum was parallel to the wall, swinging freely, never hitting an obstacle. Perhaps if it had ever been jarred enough to hit the wall something would have changed. Perhaps then, they could have moved into the stages of true intimacy with God.

Some people are like that. They live from tragedy to tragedy and never seem to hit a wall. There is a deadness inside of them that seems to be untouchable. The poor in spirit are not so. They come to the end of themselves. They ask for help. They willingly become bond slaves if need be in order to receive help. Luke could never have been a bond slave. By force of will, he would much rather continue to be a good man. Sure, he was gladly a servant of God. It was his choice. He had a large heart. He could spare some effort for God, to serve God. He could do God a favor and continue to serve Him even in tragedy. But he could not be a bond slave. Only those who reach the end of themselves can become a bond slave.

Deception of Goodness

No amount of tragedy or pain can create a bond slave. Nothing from the outside can force a person to empty himself so that he might be filled up with what God has to offer. Many choose to continue to live off their own resources, and if they can muster enough religious goodness, then their hearts can live in continual deceit of self. Their hearts can tell them of their own goodness, and deceive them into thinking they are serving God. No man can serve God without being connected to God. He may be able to deceive himself and may even deceive others. But the fruit will not lie. God is not mocked. What a man sows, that he will reap. (See Galatians 6:7–8.) If he sows to self, he will reap corruption. If He connects with God, he will bear good fruit and reap everlasting life.

Those who live in a non-intimate world are in a type of spiritual shutdown. It will not produce good fruit, no matter how good the life seems to be. The emotionally locked heart is similar. The person shuts down emotional function and lives primarily through either the will or the intellect. While this person can still try to connect with others, there is something missing. It is like dancing with a mannequin. It will be a life without power; a life without godly fruit.

Breaking through these self-made walls is one of the most difficult challenges in ministry. In fact, much of effective ministry is having the wisdom to know when the walls are finally weakening and having the patience to wait for that time. Yet, for some, the time will never come unless there is clear, focused prayer and ministry. The tendency to defend the fortress of self is the greatest enemy we face in ministry. When the fortress has been penetrated, the spirit of the person is open—at least temporarily. The time for ministry is now. The wise will move quickly and effectively during those seasons.

Why brokenness? The answer is not in the heart of God. The answer is in us. Our tendency to resist God and depend on self creates negatives, which in turn brings the pain that will bring brokenness. Most of the time, I doubt that God even needs to actively resist the hard of heart. Their own works will come back on their heads soon enough. The pain will be there. But will the brokenness? Perhaps we need to forget "Why brokenness?" and ask a smarter question: "What will it take to get us to truly connect with the heart of God?"

> *Lord Jesus, I thank You that when I am weak, then I am strong. I thank You that when I come to the end of myself, Your power is released to flow. Teach me wisdom that I might see my need for You much more quickly. Amen. (Prayer based on 2 Corinthians 12:9.)*

Study Guide

1. What are some of the paradoxes of Scripture? How is brokenness a paradox?

2. In Jesus' mission statement, what are some of the words that let us know His target of ministry? What should be our target in ministry?

3. What are the two great tendencies of the heart? How do these tendencies block out the ministry that would come from God?

4. When God is trying to bring change, how do we typically react to Him? Why do we respond this way?

5. Why do the relatively righteous struggle producing good spiritual fruit? What is it that God needs from us to produce good fruit?

6. If it is not actually brokenness itself that God wants, what does God actually want from us?

7. Where in your life do you see areas of emotional or spiritual shutdown? What kind of healing or strengthening does God want to do in those areas?

Chapter 8

THE REAL DEAL

A television commercial popularized the idea of "Talk to the hand." A teenager is caught up in his video games when the adult enters the room. The child, never missing a beat on his video games, holds his arm up with his palm facing the adult and says, "Talk to the hand, because I'm not listening."

A person living in any of the first three stages of behavior is effectively saying to God, "Talk to the hand." He may not know he is saying that to God. He may even be using religious jargon and may be making a good-flesh effort to serve God. So how can the good flesh person be saying to God, "Talk to the hand"?

It is all a matter of focus. Like the teenager focused on the video game, we can only have one focus. We either focus on the video game, or we stop and listen to what the adult has to say. I know many young people who would try to say that it is possible to do both at the same time. And yes, it is, but we are not talking about a halfhearted effort here. We are talking about serving God.

The person who tries to serve God with a divided focus will fall short of the glory of God. He will fall short of what God has planned for his life. As long as a person has a sense of "I can do this," he will have a divided focus. "I can do this" is what good flesh is all about. It strokes our egos to think we can serve God, that we can be good and get the job done. When we don't get the job done, we fall into burnout and eventually into bad flesh. All three of these stages are about human effort. All three are saying to God, "Talk to the hand. I am busy trying to be good."

Things finally begin to change when we hit that point of realizing we cannot make it without God. In 1 Peter 5:5, we get an expanded version of James 4:6 quoted in the last chapter, "Likewise you younger people, submit yourselves to your elders. Yes, all of you be submissive to one another, and be clothed with humility, for 'God resists the proud, but gives grace to the humble.'"

Pay attention to that main phrase, "God resists the proud, but gives grace to the humble." A person who thinks he can serve God without the help of God is proud, and God resists the proud. A person who realizes that he can't make it without God is beginning to move into humility, and God gives help to the humble. This is the key to moving into the behavior of stages four and five.

When a person is in the behavior of stages one, two, or three, he is effectively telling God to "Talk to the hand" because of his "I can do it by myself" attitude. When a person finally comes to the end of himself, he effectively says to God, "Come to the hand, because I need You. I need You now!"

Stage 4

Stage four begins when a person finally responds to his pain in a way that is not blaming or self-justifying. When the fire of sin has burned through the camp and all that is left is charred ashes, some still manage to return to the old cycles. They return to one of the stages of flesh. Some finally get an honest look at things, take a deep breath, and admit, "I need help." Those are beautiful words to God. After all, He created us to need Him. He created us to be vessels of His presence. We need Him in order to function properly.

When we finally say, "I need help," we are close to moving into the place that God has created especially for us. How can we be so perverse as to think that God has enjoyed watching us go through the pain? When we are close to inviting Him in, it is a joyous time for God. It is joyous for His sake and for ours. He will finally get to enjoy us because we invite Him to be present with us. He loves that communion. He will also finally get to enjoy us because we are about to move out of the flesh and into a much better life. He enjoys watching us experience real life for the first time, and He enjoys watching us produce good fruit!

"I need help" are beautiful words to God.

That is what God sees when He sees a humble heart. That is why He is drawn to a humble heart. Purpose and joy and life are getting close. I believe God is almost giddy to see this happen. He loves us that much. He is a doting Father, who is watching and waiting for that substance of humility that will invite Him in.

Stage four is the stage of true brokenness or humility. Stage four, like stage two, tends to be brief. Some artificially stay at a point of brokenness and prolong stage four. When that happens, it is a combination of stage one and stage four. These people think that by their own self-condemnation, they are beginning to move into humility. Actually, that is a lie. Anything starting with the word *self* will go back to a stage one, human-effort activity. Stage four is not about human activity. It is not about meditating on having done wrong. It is simply about seeing, owning, and getting to a point of helplessness. Those who think they can help the situation by beating themselves up are not at a point of helplessness. They are sort of recognizing the truth, but again responding with the wrong spirit. Self is very much at the center of stage one. It is not at the center of stage four.

Stage four is coming to a quiet helplessness that invites God in. This is the switch that starts the receiving process. It is the connecting to God and the receiving from God that is life. God comes to those who receive Him. Period. That's it. Stage one can't receive Him. Stage two can't receive Him. Stage three can't receive Him. Only stage four invites Him in. The wise learn to move to stage four without having to dwell in the other stages. The wise man doesn't have to be beaten to a pulp to come to a place of brokenness, humility, and helplessness. The wise man sees his need to receive continually from God and develops a lifestyle of seeking to receive from God.

Stage 5

Stage five is life in the Spirit. It is a person living in obedience, empowered by God. This person is not brittle. He knows his own limitations. He knows that without God he will fail. He lives for a season in dependency, connected and empowered. There is joy; there is peace; there is fruit.

It would be nice if the story ended there, but it doesn't. When a person begins to walk in the Spirit, he is energized. He is refreshed. His natural man is rejuvenated—which is an open invitation to return to stage one. It is our greatest tendency, now that we are living in a fallen state. As soon as there is any hope of getting it right on our own, we vacate God and His presence and begin to try to duplicate with our own efforts what He was doing through us in the intimacy stage. We return to stage one. We cease to depend on His presence to produce good fruit and instead return to human effort. We begin to live in good flesh, and generally don't even notice that the power of the Spirit has departed. We see our good actions and we are happy. It looks like God is with us. We are fulfilled until we begin to hit burnout. Not realizing what is happening, we blame others, become brittle, and start the cycle all over again.

(The completed life cycle looks as shown on the next page.)

Even the most godly person will go through brief times in each of the stages, including the flesh stages. The ungodly may never hit stage five, but especially will continue to play in stages one through three. Because we are moving from stage to stage, we think we are making progress or that we are falling back, but mostly we are playing on the stage of our own fleshly substance. The only exception is the one who is finally connecting with, and staying connected with, God.

Most of the Christian world lives under the illusion that good flesh is godliness, and then wonders why they keep falling into patterns of sin. The reality for many is that they never left the patterns of sin. They just moved into good flesh.

There are at least some advantages to good flesh, especially over bad flesh. A habit of going to church just might help a person get connected to God. Caring actions done in human effort are still caring

The Life Cycle

Man in the Image of God
Connected and Empowered

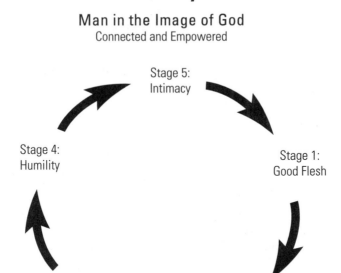

Stage 5:
Intimacy

Stage 4:
Humility

Stage 1:
Good Flesh

Stage 3:
Bad Flesh

Stage 2:
Burnout/Passive Sin

Selfish and Isolated
The Image of Man Without God

actions. They may not produce the eternal fruit of God in a person, but they at least are not creating the devastation of a drug habit.

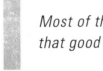

Most of the Christian world lives under the illusion that good flesh is godliness.

I am not saying that good flesh and bad flesh are equal, just that they are of similar spiritual substance. The person who has continually made attempts at caring does seem to have an easier time actually walking with God once the presence comes. The only problem is that the person who has a relatively righteous lifestyle seldom sees the need for God's presence. Hence the need for God to allow that person to go through times of testing to move them to the point of inviting in the presence of God.

We would never let it happen that way. We love our good flesh too much. We want God to help us step from good flesh to godliness, from human effort to God-empowered actions and words. Unfortunately, the pathway to godliness is through humility, not through a confidence in our good flesh.

Seeking God Through Sin

So what about Bill, the guy who felt closer to God once he had a few beers? Bill was a perfectionist. A definite stage one junky. He had a lifestyle of pressing for the best possible performance in that good flesh area of human effort. All of that pressing had shut God out so tightly, Bill had no hope of experiencing God's presence while in his righteous mode. At least, he thought it was his righteous mode. It wasn't until he began to break down that he would drink. Under the influence, he could finally mellow, but it was a mellowing with a tinge of conviction. That sounds a little bit like humility doesn't it? Maybe, just maybe, there was enough stage four present that he was feeling some of the presence of God.

Unfortunately, the Bills of this world are in more danger than they realize. If the alcohol mellows them, it is dangerously close to becoming addictive, especially if that person is someone who presses himself to the point of burnout. Not only that, if he begins to equate a sense of good feeling with the alcohol, and misses the real cause of any true good feeling, he is really in trouble. He will turn to alcohol to seek the presence and miss the true pathway of humility. Actually, it was the little bit of conscience that was mixed in that was bringing the potential connection, not the drink itself.

I have seen people who seem to walk consciously into sin as a way to try to find God. Since they only feel close to God after a binge of bad flesh, they just go off the deep end for a season as a way to try to find God. After the binge comes the repentance. Then comes the time of presence. After a few of these cycles, the person begins to associate the sin binge with the presence that comes later, and in a foolish way begins to depend on the sin cycle with its repentance as the way to God. This person lives from incredible high to incredible low. It is an inconsistent and sick lifestyle, and does not bring glory to God. It is the humility that is the key—not the drinking, not the sin binge. Wisdom learns the humility pathway without having to be stupid. Only a fool thinks that a good pathway to God is through grotesque sin.

However, the true addiction for most people is not the alcohol, but the good flesh. I have known many revival chasers over the years. They are always looking for that one secret, for that one touch from God that will put them over the top; that will break some bondage that they struggle with and finally bring them to perfection. They hope for some connection with God that will bring an inner sense that they are meeting the standard, and that their efforts have finally arrived. *Having arrived* ... that sounds to me very much like they are chasing good flesh—only they don't know that they are chasing good flesh. They think they are chasing a great outpouring of God.

During moments of spiritual ecstasy, they have a temporary illusion of having arrived. Next they go into the brittle stage of effort, and then they crash or go chase some new revival movement. There is a continual thirst to find some experience that will create a permanent sense of being whole. The only place of being whole that God offers is to be continually dependent on Him. It is in our weakness that we find His strength.

The wise man can actually jump across the diagram from good flesh to humility, if he learns to see his good flesh for what it is. This is depicted in a more complex diagram of the cycles that includes both this possibility and the possibility of bouncing from stage one to stage three and back again:

The Life Cycle
Man in the Image of God
Connected and Empowered

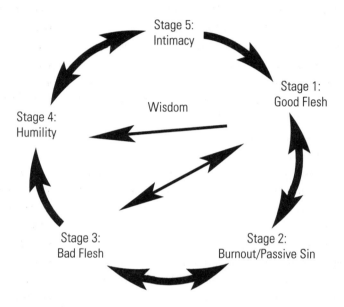

Selfish and Isolated
The Image of Man Without God

Tim's Story

Tim went from a drug-induced high to a spiritual high in the space of a few hours. His parents had been working on him for years, and he finally gave in to Christ. It was as if the speaker was speaking directly to his heart. He knew he had heard from God. The power of God touched him and he was clean. Forever clean.

The party scene had been good. Tim loved the flair and the fun. It had given him the cover he needed to take no responsibility. He could be impulsive, controlling, the center of attention, and spaced out. He could be and do just about anything, which was a far cry from the negative view of religion that he had inherited from his parents. During his growing up years, God had been about rules and restrictions. It had cramped his style and he had no use for it.

But this was different. This spiritual high was incredible. Somehow, he'd had it all wrong. God wasn't the killjoy that he thought He was. This was better than any high he'd ever had. It was an emotional and spiritual rush beyond compare. Why hadn't he seen it before?

In time, the initial high in God began to fade. Like most people, Tim's first experiences were very formative, and Tim set up a kind of narrow view of how God works that mimicked his own experience. Tim had found God at a revival meeting. He had come to a revival meeting and there, listening to the words of an anointed man, he'd found God. So the search began. It was a search that would go on for years. Tim was continually out there looking for the latest wave, the current place of God's presence. He wanted to be at the place of the smack of the kiss of God. He craved it. Who was more spiritually hungry than Tim?

It all looked so good to the public, but there were a few facts that just did not seem to line up with the fruit of God. His wife and children felt continually alienated and neglected. To Tim, this was a bit of a martyr's badge. He was spiritually hungry, and she was not. How could he help it if she did not get the same level of spiritual satisfaction out of pursuing God that he did? But it was not just his wife that felt it. Tim always seemed to have a need to be in control, to be at the center. In addition, those who tried to connect with him found it difficult. It was possible to hang around him and listen to his ponderings, but it never quite felt like it was a real heart that was coming forth.

There came a day when the weight of real life finally caught up with him. Depression was setting in, and he was on the verge of having an affair. It was time for real action. Since he could not find a revival that would seem to quench his thirst, he took matters into his own hands. He headed for the ministry, an outreach to people who had been as he had been before he found Christ—a ministry to those caught up in addictions.

Again, there was a sense of success for a season as he threw himself into the middle of the work. But it was hard work. Too many of them just didn't get it. Why couldn't they be like him? When the anointing was present, these things should break. He worked endless hours until his energy waned. Then it snapped. He couldn't go one more day. He walked out on it all and headed for a mundane job, one that would require no thought, no energy, nothing. Just time alone. The God thing wasn't working, and he didn't know what else to do.

Beers and "Anointing"

Like Bill, Tim was in dangerous territory. Bill sought the anointing through a few beers. Tim was trying to find God in the right place of anointing, the right service. That can be dangerous. When that didn't work, he tried to be the place of anointing himself. That too was a disaster. Incidentally, after crashing for a season, Tim's natural man was renewed, and he jumped back into the ministry again. This time, when he was on the verge of crashing, there was a sympathetic "spiritual" woman waiting to hear his story. This time the outcome was tragic.

Tim never saw the cycles. He could not be talked out of the fact that it was as much his natural man that was being stimulated as his spiritual man. He knew he had heard from God and he would not even consider listening to anything else. That kind of hardness is the perfect illustration of the brittle aspect of stage one.

James 3:17 says it this way, "But the wisdom that is from above is first pure, then peaceable, gentle, willing to yield, full of mercy and good fruits, without partiality and without hypocrisy." Something that is truly of God's Spirit has a "willing to yield" quality that is not present in a human-effort imitation of the Spirit. A godly man may choose to stand his ground under the direction of the Spirit, but He does so with a soft, compassionate, and yielded heart. The ungodly are brittle, divisive, insistent on their way, and often at the center of their own way.

Tim couldn't see the absolute lack of intimacy and connection to God or man. There had been a deep wounding that had shut him down and so the only thing that could seem to give him life was the flash and the fire. And so much the better if he was at the center. It was that way in the party life. It was that way in the spiritual life. The louder and crazier the spiritual environment, the better it felt, until finally that was not enough. So he tried to be the minister. Still, he lacked life because he lacked connection.

Blaming Others

For a brief time, he was at a point when I thought he might see what was happening. He was open and honest and then just as quickly he turned on me. I was bringing him pain. I had to be wrong. In retrospect, I think he spiritually equated me to the "browbeating" he got from his parents before he started his revival quests. He felt some of the same kind of negative pressure from his wife. She too eventually became the enemy.

That is the problem when a person doesn't understand the stages. People become the enemy because they are "causing" failure. Blaming others for failure is almost certain evidence that a person is in the stage one area of depending on human strength. Blaming or controlling behaviors serve as a cover for the ego and allow the person to maintain the illusion of progress. Then when the energy runs out and the passive or complacent manner kicks in, there is a time of confusion and hopelessness. Tim hit that, but reached the wrong conclusion. He went back to stage one and retried human effort, all the while thinking he was reconnecting with the revival flow.

Incidentally, a minister who is moving in a human effort flow can be very successful for a season. It is intoxicating to the flesh to be inspired to effort in the good flesh area. A person who is full of spiritual pride can trigger that pride in others, and spiritual pride can stir a burst of natural energy and activity that will appear to be a great effort for Christ. When a collective burnout comes, it should be obvious that at least the majority of the work was not energized by Christ. Most of the time, we miss that fact.

When pride bears fruit in the form of division, it also should be obvious that the spiritual substance was not a connectedness to

Christ. Those in pride love the preeminence. Two people who love the preeminence eventually will not be able to get along, thus the division. Division is a fruit of spiritual pride. In contrast, those connected to Christ will be "willing to yield" and will be able to walk in unity. If Tim had been honest about the trail of fruit in his family and his ministry, he could have made some adjustments. Instead, he kept returning to stage one, thinking that he was pursuing God.

For a season, people did flock to Tim and his ministry. He had the illusion of success until it all came crashing down. Who knows the spiritual wreckage that he left behind when he crashed in grotesque sin? The minister who is inspiring good flesh will have this kind of legacy. There will be a great fire for a season, and then a whole lot of ash and soot.

Fruit doesn't lie.

Fruit doesn't lie. Given time for the initial flash of the good flesh effort to fade, the fruit that remains will always tell the true story. It will reveal the difference between the one walking in good flesh, and the one truly walking in Christ. Tim came so close, but refused to face the pain and returned to the blame game. It was everybody else. He had heard from God. He knew the source of life and was right.

Revival chasers are often classic illustrations of people who don't understand the stages. They think there is only one solution: connect with God in the fire. In a way they are right, but they miss the pathway. They look for God in a place, in a man, in a movement, or in a set of actions. But God only is found in one specific place—the place of brokenness. It is a different kind of fire than the revival chaser sees. It is the place of humility; a place that recognizes that God is God and invites Him to be Lord. All else merely glorifies human effort.

Do you want the real deal—or are you willing to settle for human effort? Is your palm facing outward saying to God "Talk to the hand?" Or are you ready to lift your hands in surrender and say, "God, I desperately need you now?" God has so much more for us than most believers ever experience. I hope that you will settle for nothing less than the real deal—a life of intimacy with Christ.

> *Jesus, I am ready for the real thing. I don't want any impostors. I want to know that I know that I am in You. I know that if I come to You as a child, You will hear and answer my prayers. God, pour Your Holy Spirit into my life. Amen. (Prayer based on Luke 18:17, 11:13.)*

Study Guide

1. What two things have to stop for a person to move into stage four?

2. Describe the final two stages in your own words.

3. When we turn to humility, why does it bring joy to the heart of God?

4. What is the typical response after a person reaches intimacy with God? Why is intimacy with God so hard to maintain?

5. Some people actually do find a pathway to God through grotesque sin. How can this happen? How can this negative pathway become almost addictive to the person?

6. Most of the time, a revival chaser is actually chasing what? How does a person know if he is genuinely seeking God or chasing an illusion?

7. Give some illustrations of times when you were in each of the stages.

Chapter 9

FROM THE IMAGE OF DUST

And as we have borne the image of the man of dust, we shall also bear the image of the heavenly Man.
—1 Corinthians 15:49

Magnets line up with the north-south axis. Oil floats on water. Hot air rises. As human beings, our natural resting place is good flesh. We go there without thinking, without effort. It just happens. Why is good flesh so natural to us?

Ironically enough, the place of good flesh is the place of our gifting. Sure, some of the time our good flesh is nothing more than the habits we have acquired from those around us. As human beings, we certainly are shaped by our environment. But there also is a very strong, invisible pull that has little or nothing to do with how our environment has shaped us. Any parent with more than one child can tell you that each child is his own person. There may be one environment, but there are many outcomes.

Psalm 139 clearly tells us that our invisible part, our inner nature, comes complete with many tendencies that were formed before we ever took on a physical body. God saw each one of us before we ever existed and placed us into this life at a specific point in time. We are not an accident any more than the order of nature is an accident.

Good flesh is simply our attempt to be what God created us to be, except that we are doing it without God.

If that is true, why would God allow our good flesh to be such a strong pull, such a natural tendency in our lives? Why wouldn't He create us with the desire to do His will, to complete the calling He has for each one of us? The answer is: He has. It is called *good flesh.*

From the point that Adam sinned, the holy God whom we love and serve had to take a step back from mankind. Pure holiness cannot draw near to sin without expressing some form of judgment. It is a consistent principle in Scripture that the closer God draws to man, the greater the judgment. Similarly, the more distant He remains, the more judgment is delayed. With Adam's fall, God's mercy required Him to distance Himself, so that He might give man the time to humble himself and return to the living God.

Good flesh is simply our attempt to be what God created us to be—except, we are doing it without God. It is Abraham's Ishmael. When Abraham's desire for a child was not fulfilled quickly enough by God for Abraham, he turned to his handmaid to father a child. Wrong plan. That was a good flesh attempt to have a child. And the world is still experiencing the consequences of that one good flesh act!

Good flesh is also Moses killing the Egyptian while he was still in the palace in Egypt. In Acts 7:25, it explains that Moses killed the man, thinking that the Israelites would know that God had raised him up to deliver his people from Egypt. He knew that was his purpose. He acted. Instead of being the inaugural act of his ministry, it sent him fleeing for his life to the backside of a desert. Good flesh will do that. And time after time, we are confused by the outcome of our good flesh actions, because we too suppose that everyone should recognize that we are "the deliverer of Israel." We too have a destiny that pulls us into living the best way we know how, and those actions come back to slap us in the face.

Mere Dust or Glorious?

From the time that Adam sinned, God distanced Himself from man. Man without God is mere dust. There is no meaning. There is no purpose. There is no glory. That is what the verse in 1 Corinthians 15:49 means. We have "borne the image of the man of dust." We have experienced what it means to live without God, and that image is what I call the good flesh. Sure, some turn to evil and live an even more grotesque form of their being dust (stage three behavior), but for most, the continual resting place is good flesh.

We can despair over our good flesh, or we can begin to see that it is the place of our gifting, our calling, and then work to transform it to its intended purpose. Abraham did eventually have the son of the promise, Isaac, by Sarah. Moses did eventually deliver Israel. But both had to wait on God, and neither could do what he was called to do without his dust being transformed by the power of God into His very image. We have borne the image of dust, but God wants us to "bear the image of the heavenly Man!"

Our good-flesh resting place does not need to be a place of despair, but a place of hope. It is a clue to our calling. It provides insight into the spiritual gifts God has given us. We just need God's understanding to know what the dust will look like once God has breathed on it. From Ishmael to Isaac, from murder to deliverer, there is a huge difference between the two. One will produce life. One will result in death. The difference is the breath of God.

Seeing Our Gifts Through Our Spiritual Flows

The easiest place to see this is in the area of spiritual flows that I introduced in chapter 4. Though we could list hundreds of subtle variations, there are seven negative flows that summarize what we look like when we depart from the presence of God and demonstrate the dust of the good flesh:

1. Pride
2. Fear

3. Rebellion
4. Lust
5. Bitterness
6. Critical spirit
7. Selfish ambition

Most people can spot at least one of the above flows as being present or even being dominant during different seasons of their lives. What the life cycle diagram illustrates is that these flows are likely more dominant than we realized. They are present in both the good flesh and the burnout/passive sin stages as well as in the bad flesh.

That's the bad news. The good news is that these same flows also point us in the direction of the call of God. Most would see a word like *pride* and try to say that the godly parallel would be the opposite, which would be humility. Unfortunately, it doesn't work that way. The proud person will never have a natural inclination toward humility.

Actually, how it works is illustrated by the term *core values*. Each of these flows represents a core value that has been planted in the individual by God. We have within us a deep desire to do the very things He has called us to do. It is at the very heart of our being. However, instead of it showing up in its pure form that would demonstrate the image and glory of God, it shows up in the image of dust. Only the presence of God can produce the image of God. The best man can do without God's presence is good flesh.

Because of our core values, we will strive to be that man or woman God has created us to be. Birds fly. Fish swim. And men slide into their calling in some form, whether in good flesh, bad flesh, or in a way that brings forth the very image of God. The good flesh reveals our core values and our natural abilities that God has placed in each of us. Below is a list of the natural values and abilities for each of the seven negative flows:

- Pride: Caring about the opinions of others, responsibility, leadership ability

- Fear: Focus, imagination, vision, direction-setting

- Rebellion: Initiative, creativity, strength

- Lust: Ability to value, give a sense of value to others

- Bitterness: Sensitivity, caring for others, connecting

- Critical spirit: Discernment, ability to see right and wrong

- Selfish ambition: Ability to focus on accomplishments, goals, attention to detail

Some of the parallel abilities and values are a bit difficult to see until we better understand the concept of core values. A person's greatest pain will be in the area of his highest sense of value. Bitterness is a great example. One would think that the bitter person has little or no capacity for relationship. Instead, bitterness is actually an indicator that the person places a high value on relationship. The more deeply we care about something, the more deeply we can be hurt. Those who are intensely bitter must have had a high value on relationship or the pain would not have been great enough to create the highly negative response.

In the same way, the person who values faith, vision, and a future orientation likely will struggle with fear. The basic ability of this person is to visualize. A person who is capable at visualizing can imagine good things for the future (faith) or he can imagine bad things for the future (fear). The same gift can be dust or it can be the very image of God. A visionary person can create his own visions that seem to have a positive twist (good flesh vision). He also can be dominated by worry (passive sin). He can visualize very vain things or even things that are hurtful to others (bad flesh). These are all dust. But there is something better. God intends for us to connect with Him, to get His vision for the future, and to respond as a faith partner with Him, seeing His intended future and praying it into existence.

Abraham did that, with a slight detour during the time of Ishmael. Moses, too, saw God's intended future and began to pursue it in his own strength. Both of these men demonstrated the dust part of the picture and both of them also demonstrated what it means to be turned into the image of the heavenly man.

Every one of the spiritual flows is like that. They all have good flesh, burnout or passive flesh, and bad flesh forms. But they also have the potential of being transformed into the very image of God and the transforming agent is the presence of God. More often than not, what keeps us from connecting to God is not the bad flesh, or even the burnout, but our faith in the good flesh. As long as we can make our dust look good, we usually can be O.K. with it. I believe that "good" is our greatest enemy of godliness.

Godliness is established when we allow God to take our pride and transform it into leadership that is buffered by humility. Again, most people make the mistake of trying to change a bad flow into its opposite. Instead, we need to see the core value of the flow, and then nurture the release of that core value in the way that God would desire. A prideful person cares about the opinions of others. That is not necessarily a bad thing. In Christ, that value translates into servant leadership. The person still cares about the opinions of others and is attentive to what might help motivate or move them in the right direction. That's leadership. In the dust form, pride cares more about its own reputation than the purposes of God.

Because of the controlling core value, a leadership person will struggle with pride, and a pride person will have the potential to be a good leader. The dust and the image of God are one and the same. One lacks the presence of God and the other is elevated and empowered by the Spirit of God into His very image.

Too many people hate themselves or their families because of a controlling spiritual flow that has dominated the generations.

Too many people hate themselves or their families because of a controlling spiritual flow that has dominated the generations. Bitterness often dominates entire family groups for hundreds of years.

In this model, what would that tell us about that family? It tells us that God had put a strong call on that family to excellence in the area of relationship. Yes, I believe that entire families and even nations are called in specific areas. If a family or a nation walks without God, they will not fulfill their destiny. In a way, they likely might fulfill a version of their destiny. They will walk out the dust form of their calling, but they will never demonstrate the goodness and glory of God as He had intended.

Causing People to Question God

The bitter family walks around with a level of woundedness that is frightening, causing people to begin to question the goodness of God. This is what it means in Romans 1:18, when it says, "For the wrath of God is revealed from heaven against all ungodliness and unrighteousness of men, who suppress the truth in unrighteousness." Man was created to reveal the goodness and the glory of God to the world. For man to do that, he must connect with God and release His life into the world. Otherwise, all that can be seen is the dust image, and the truth about the goodness of God is suppressed.

Every time a person begins to connect with God and to walk in the image of God, he is demonstrating the goodness of God to a dead and dying world. This life is not about demonstrating good works. It is very possible for good works to be a good flesh effort, an effort which actually hides the goodness of God, and which will eventually decay into its passive sin and bad flesh cousins.

While God will reward those who choose to walk with Him, it is not just our rewards that are at stake. It is the reputation of God and ultimately the souls of men that are at stake. When we refuse to connect with God and to release His image into the world, we suppress the truth of God and the resulting darkness only increases the chance that men will see God as an angry and judging God who is not safe to approach. That is where our disobedience translates into the loss of souls. We hide the truth of God's goodness and His mercy. His goodness and mercy endures forever, but when we shrink back, we hide His goodness.

Romans 1:19 says, "What may be known of God is manifest in them, for God has shown it to them." Notice what it says. What may be known of God is manifest in us. It is there in seed form. We may be perverting it. But God is continually wooing us toward that place where He wants us to walk. Our good flesh, that natural resting place, is an arrow pointing us in the right direction. Our good flesh does not have to be a millstone hanging around our necks. Instead it can be a sign of hope and of His calling.

The pride person is called to leadership. The fear person is called to demonstrate faith. The rebel has great creativity and strength. The one who lusts has the ability to give others a sense of value. The bitter person has the potential for quality relationships. The critical person has a great ability to discern and guard the truth. The person who is full of selfish ambition is a go-getter and can become a peacemaker by focusing everyone on a common goal.

Knowing that a person's greatest struggles are merely the dust side of the very image of God for that person is very liberating!

Understanding core values is the key to seeing and releasing the will of God in a person's life. Knowing that a person's greatest struggles are merely the dust side of the very image of God for that person is very liberating! Who struggles more than the bitter person? But his bitterness is a key to his future happiness in Christ. He simply needs to learn to forgive, and to walk in a way that honors and values his relationships. That will bring a sense of fulfillment to the bitter person. It will fulfill his destiny.

It is hard to believe that water, ice, and steam are all the same substance, but it is true. It is hard to believe that bitterness and mercy come out of the same core value, but it is true. God is capable of bringing radical transformation into the lives of individuals, families, and even nations. Sometimes, that transformation just happens, but I have found that where there is vision, the transformation is much easier.

As lifegivers, it is our responsibility to learn to see people as God intends them to be. We have to be able to see past the ugly exterior of the flesh and visualize the godly end He intends. In some cases, we have to see past the angel of light exterior of the good flesh for progress to be made. Man tends to look on the outward appearance and is often fooled by a false, angelic glow. God looks on the heart and is never fooled.

As we learn to walk with God, we too can see what God sees. We too can learn to see the heart. We can see the good and the bad, but more importantly, we can see God's intended end. Through the eyes of faith, we can see His image established in every man.

That is the heart of the intercessor. This kind of vision will change lives. Start with yourself. Can you see His image developing? As we learn to see His image coming out of the dust, we are beginning to release the life of God into our world.

> *My God and my Father, I ask You to transform my thinking. I have often seen darkness and hopelessness and despair. I have judged others. I have judged myself. I have prayed without hope and without faith. Forgive me. I want to see Your will and Your plans for me and for others. Help me to pray with Your vision so that I can prove that good and acceptable and perfect will You have for each one of us. Amen. (Prayer based on Romans 12:2.)*

Study Guide

1. The chapter states that the place of good flesh is the place of our gifting. Explain what is meant by that statement and give examples.

2. How do both Moses and Abraham illustrate a person performing his call with a good flesh effort?

3. As you look over the negative spiritual flows, are there any that tend to be the most dominant in your life? What does that tell you about a possible call of God on your life?

4. How can a bitter person actually be a person who places a high value on people? What concept illustrates that a bitter person has to be a people person?

5. For each of the spiritual flows, what is the key to transforming them to "the image of the heavenly Man?" In the case of bitterness, how is that activated?

6. How does whether or not we walk in the image of God effect the reputation of God?

7. What new vision have you gained for your life through this chapter? What new vision have you gained for someone that you are ministering to?

Chapter 10

TURNING OBSTACLES INTO PEARLS

For months we fought with an office fax machine. The office equipment people told us the machine was fine, so we talked to the phone company. The phone company told us the line was fine and that it was the machine. We tried everything, even getting a new machine. One day, I moved the fax into my office, attaching it with a different phone cord. It worked. I did not know whether to be frustrated or happy. A phone line that seemingly worked for everything else would not work for the fax. I still don't really know why. A cheap, single-line wire worked. So, we just keep the fax connected to that same wire. It works! That's good enough for me.

For most people, life is a little bit like that. If it works, don't mess with it. The problem is that often it really is not working that well. With our fax, it would work about one out of every three times. Of course, when we really needed it, it seemed like it worked about one out of every twenty tries. Higher stress seems to keep even a machine from working!

Passing Vision and Value

The greatest tools for a lifegiver are those things that pass vision and value through a heart of faith to another person. For that to happen, there must be a clear connection established. The phone line can't be messed up. The receiver has to be working. Anyone who has worked in the area of person-to-person communication knows the difficulty of keeping the lines open and clear. According to what we have studied in a spiritual substance worldview, any kind of negative spiritual substance will likely create some interference. John 3:20–21 explains this fact:

> For everyone practicing evil hates the light and does not come to the light, lest his deeds should be exposed. But he who does the truth comes to the light, that his deeds may be clearly seen, that they have been done in God.

These verses speak of the evil person hating and being afraid of the Light. If a person is clothed with the presence of God, he represents the Light. He is likely to become the object of scorn of the evil person.

This is a problem for the lifegiver. This is a problem for the one who desires to witness for Christ. The very thing that empowers him to be a witness or an intercessor is the very thing that makes him repulsive to the person in need. That is a definite obstacle.

Add to that one other complicating factor: people tend to hear according to their heart. They will apply filters to everything that is said according to their worldview, which is largely determined by their substance within. Thus, any comments made to the unsaved are likely to be misinterpreted. The phone lines are down; there is maybe a one-in-three chance of getting through. But then again, if the need is high—if there is stress—it is more like a one-in-twenty chance.

Relationship Accesses Substance

So how do we begin to improve our odds of a good connection? The answer is relationship. *Relationship* is a broad and varied word. There are about as many approaches to relationship as there are people. And that is the secret—every person is a combination of both good and evil. In Luke 6:45, it tells us that, "A good man out of the good treasure of his heart brings forth good; and an evil man out of the evil treasure of his heart brings forth evil. For out of the abundance of the heart his mouth speaks." When I first read this verse, I saw the good man as having a good heart and the bad man as having a bad heart. That is not what the verse says. It says "out of the good treasure" the man brings forth good. A good man is not described as being completely and purely good, but instead he learns to access the good and leave the bad alone.

Even so, through relationship, we can learn to access the different substances of a person's heart. Every person has a key or keys to connectedness. There are some people who are so immersed in darkness that those keys may be hard to find. Darkness isolates. It sets itself off by itself. Spirituality is about staying connected. Thus, learning relationship is very close to learning spirituality. There is a soulish realm to relationship that is not entirely spiritual, but true relationship cannot happen apart from a genuine connection, which requires a spiritual exchange. We can communicate mind-to-mind or emotion-to-emotion, but that is not nearly as fulfilling as spiritually connecting with another person. It is the spiritual connection that gives a sense of intimacy, of fullness to a relationship.

Almost all obstacles to ministry are those things that shut down our ability to connect with another person. Any negative substance is the first obstacle. It causes people to want to run from the light. However, no man is entirely dark. The trick is to find the key to access the good part, to temporarily bring forth a presence that has the ability to connect. Sometimes that can happen through discussion of family, sometimes through work topics, or sometimes through accomplishments. Mostly, it is achieved by drawing out the core values; the heart of the other person.

After all, our greatest areas of darkness actually are nothing more than a perversion of our gifting and call. If we can learn to see past that darkness to the person's purpose, we can activate the light in him and begin to connect with him. As human beings, we respond to hope. We respond when someone sees us for who God created us to be and passes a sense of value along to us. When we learn to see the God-created part of a person, we activate the light and thus the potential for connection.

Finding Someone's Passion

Every man is created with a passion, with a set of core values that are the very essence of his being. For some, the passion is so beat down that there is little flame left. But if we can begin to see and trigger the God-created man, we will find life. Many people, even some who see themselves as ministers to others, are only able to approach others on their own terms with a selfish approach. The person who can put himself aside and value another person is much more able to create *relationship*, to *connect*, and to bring *healing*. All three of these terms describe a true presence of God transfer that will be life giving to another person.

Every man is created with a passion.

The selfish cannot get outside themselves and thus are not capable of intimacy. Two people with unforgiveness may for a time feel a sense of intimacy if they have a common enemy. Two people in rebellion, especially if both have a common point of rebellion such as toward parents, may feel a sense of connection for a time because of what they have in common. Intimacy that has at its core a connection of darkness to darkness is doomed to failure. The inner bitterness or rebellion will turn at some point on its newfound friend and destroy the fragile fabric of this connection. Only the selfless (or godly) are truly able to connect on any lasting basis.

Jesus frequently used questions to connect with people. Nicodemus was a religious ruler. (See John 3.) He came skeptical. He even came by night so as not to be recognized and hopefully not reported. With Nicodemus, Jesus played to his intellectual curiosity. It was an open door for Jesus. He asked questions that Nicodemus could not answer. In doing so, He helped bring Nicodemus to the end of himself, to a point of humility. Humility can hear Jesus. Pride cannot. Direct confrontation would have stirred pride. Hard questions triggered a part of Nicodemus that was at least able to hear and listen.

In John 4, Jesus begins talking with the woman at the well. For all practical purposes, she is a harlot; seemingly with no good substance. Why even bother trying to connect? Yet, Jesus starts her off with a request for her to draw water for Him. Immediately, her spiritual chip is triggered. Here is a man and a Jew asking for water from a Samaritan woman. She starts out with a bit of an attitude toward Jesus, but as the conversation progresses she senses she is being treated like a real human being. Here is a man who is actually talking to her, who is actually seeing some worth in her. We can see the change in her heart as the conversation progresses. She goes from taunting him about being a Jew and having nothing to draw with, to "Sir, give me this water."

The water is a conversation point. It is a safe topic. It begins to mask the dark/light contrast long enough for Jesus to begin to trigger a desire within the Samaritan woman for the life that Jesus has. That is a beautiful picture of relationship and how it works to move people toward being receptive to the light. We have to find a connecting point, some place of common ground, even if it is just questions that show interest in the other person. Initially, it is also good if the questions are in a "safe" area.

The core of relationship is finding a connecting point.

This is the core of relationship: finding a connecting point. Relationship is built around words and actions that are composed of the ordinary stuff of life, but it is not just the ordinary stuff of life. Every word spoken, every action we do carries a spiritual content. It may be an "I love you" or an "I hate this job." Words and actions have motivations and consequences. They carry attitudes and values. There is a spiritual dimension to all we do. We are constantly writing on the hearts of others and on our own hearts. If we work with a bored and listless heart, we are being transformed into that image. How we relate to others touches them as a person.

Relationship is meant to carry intimate and meaningful messages of value to others. Often, it ends up carrying messages like, "You don't matter unless you make my life better," or "You're a fun person when you respond the way I want you to." So many of our messages are self-centered.

Relationship that is other-centered is life giving. It does not have to be spiritual conversation, but it does have to trigger and eventually transfer godly presence and substance for it to be life-giving relationship. I can talk about cows, or cars, or a football game, or clothes, or shopping and convey a sense of caring. Or I can be bored. While I do point to prayer and presence as the keys to releasing life in others, life is the true vehicle of healing. Spiritual life flows through our natural bodies in the form of seemingly mundane actions.

The greatest obstacle, then, is identifying anything that would block the connections that help us to be lifegivers to one another. Perhaps the best answer for relationship killers would be sin—plain old sin. Anything that misses the mark of our created purpose, anything that smacks of darkness, is trouble.

Yet a better answer is not sin, but our inability to see through the sin to identify the God-created person. If we can see past the sin of another person and value that person for who he is, we create a connecting point. With true connection comes the possibility of releasing the life of God in and through that individual. Vision and value passed through relationship are incredible tools God has given us to transform the obstacles of sin into pearls of His glory.

Seeing From the Negative to the Positive

In the last chapter, I listed the negative spiritual flows along with the core values. That is a starting point for seeing past the negatives to God-created purpose. The following list contains the same flows with an expanded description of the potential for each negative flow:

■ Spiritual pride: Values the opinions of others, has a desire to lead, to influence others, to be a nurturer or caregiver.

- Fear: Values the ability to help shape a positive future, has the ability to focus, to be a person of vision, imagination, direction setting.

- Rebellion: Values the strength of godly authority, has the ability to take initiative, to be creative, to be a strong leader.

- Lust: Values contentment and satisfaction, desires to enjoy life with people, ability to value, to show appreciation, and to give a sense of value to others.

- Bitterness: Values quality relationships, are sensitive and caring people, capable of connecting, playing a support role to others.

- A critical spirit: Values truth and knowledge, ability to see right and wrong, gifted thinkers, able to discern the complexity of issues.

- Selfish ambition: Values accomplishments, the completion of projects, ability to focus on goals, to be directed and organized, to be attentive to details.

For each core value, we need to be able to see its strengths even if it is being expressed negatively. The rebel values the strength of godly authority and typically is a strong and creative person. These are awesome traits when expressed in the manner God desires. Elijah is given high regard as a man of God, and he definitely typifies the strong, creative, and independent type. However, if Elijah steps out from under the authority of God, his values would become warped toward selfishness, and he would become a hardhearted rebel. We get a glimpse of what Elijah looks like when not connected to God when he is running from Jezebel. He throws a bit of a spiritual temper tantrum.

It is not the core value of the man that will need to change, but how it is being expressed. In fact, the core value will likely be visible in a good flesh, burnout, or bad flesh form. Yet, it will be the very same core value that God will use to produce His fruit once the person is connected to Him. Truly, our greatest weaknesses are our greatest strengths.

One of the key messages of this book is that only by connecting with the presence of God can we truly live out an expression of the glory of God. Anyone who is disconnected from God will begin to drift toward the negative flows. Some become hardhearted and run toward evil, but most fight against it and try to be good. Those who try to be good will only slow down the drift, but there will still be a subtle downward spiral.

If we see people from that point of view, when we see the negative flows in a person's life, we think differently. We begin to think about what that person could be if he or she were only reconnected to God. When we see hatred, we see a person who is emotionally passionate, who has the potential to be a caring person. When we see a vain, egotistical person, we are looking at someone who cares about the opinions of others. Because he cares, he has the potential to be attentive to others in a way that will make him a good leader. Or, he can just continue to be vain. The difference is getting the person connected with God.

Passing Vision and Value

In order to activate real connection, we must learn to see the godly future of a person and activate the passion God has put within the individual. When we see negative spiritual flows, we are seeing a passion being expressed negatively. Nicodemus was in a critical flow. Jesus began to test his knowledge and found a connection point to his passion. The woman at the well responded to Jesus with a very sarcastic tone. It is obvious that she cared about how she was viewed by others. Jesus asked her for help and continued in a tone that respected her, yet established who He is. People who care about the opinions of others are potential leaders. The woman at the well was instrumental in positively impacting the opinions of an entire town toward Jesus.

Turning obstacles to pearls is as simple as learning to see a value center in a person and to activate that value. When we do that, we potentially connect with the person in a way that allows us to pour the life of God into the person. Sure, some who are vain will stay in their vanity. Some who are critical will remain scoffers. Connecting is not a magical toy. We are dealing with real people who must choose to embrace what is being offered. But at least something within them is being activated which gives them the chance to receive from God.

We can be put off by the grotesque forms of the gifting, or we can begin to activate the godly by seeing the God-created person. Every person who has ever lived is an illustration of this principle. Joseph could be seen as an arrogant dreamer, but demonstrated godly leadership under Pharaoh. Gideon was a very fear-dominated person, but when he used his ability to focus positively, he took on insurmountable odds. Jonah ran from the command of God, but once he submitted, he stood up to one of the great kings.

For every man alive, his good flesh and bad flesh are nothing more than varying expressions of the passion God has put on the inside. God allows the obstacles of life to bring people up short, to let them know that they are not adequate in and of themselves to handle life. It is at those times that most people are open to connection. They are open to the person who will value them and begin to give them a sense of vision.

If that happens, an obstacle has the potential of being turned into a pearl. Just as a natural pearl is formed when a secretion surrounds something like a grain of sand that is an irritant, so a spiritual pearl forms when the presence of God covers an irritation in a person's life. Unfortunately, in many cases, the one who is irritated pushes away the presence of God. Without His presence, instead of a pearl forming, there is only the product of an irritated life.

From Irritation to Understanding

Often, we become more capable of responding positively when we understand that the irritants of life may be nothing more than God's response to our spiritual flow. Below is a list of the flows with God's responses as seen in Scripture to each flow:

- Spiritual pride: Makes the person wait, resists him (James 4:6).

- Fear and unbelief: Nurtures the person (Matt. 6:25–34).

- Rebellion: Crushes him (Prov. 29:1).

- Lust: Commands him to stop, to flee from it (2 Tim. 2:22).

- Bitterness: Isolates it (Matt. 18:35).

- Critical spirit: Contends with it (Matt. 23:1–36).

- Selfish Ambition: Gives him over to pursuit (Ps. 106:15).

People often feel like they are "the only one" to go through their kind of trauma. They think they are being singled out. The reality is that both God and man tend to react to negative flows in a similar manner. We back off from the bitter person, leaving him isolated. We instinctively contend with a critical spirit. We resist the proud.

As long as a person is able to blame others for his miseries in life, he is not owning the spiritual flow that he is putting out toward others. Nor is he seeing life through the lens of sowing and reaping. What we sow, we will also reap. The law of sowing and reaping is an impersonal force like the law of gravity.

Once a person starts to see his irritations as more of an impersonal force, he is more likely to be willing to cooperate with that force and to live in a manner to begin to benefit from that force. Instead, many see God and this life as haphazard in nature. To them, it seems that all the wrong breaks seem to be landing on them. That is not the

God that we serve. He is just and will reward those who seek Him according to His Word and His ways.

Cooperating With God

The key is learning to cooperate with God to see the negative transformed to the positive. For each of the flows, there is a transforming response that will move the person from darkness to light, from good flesh to godliness. Here are the transforming responses:

- Spiritual pride: Actively wait on God, take on service roles.

- Fear and unbelief: Get vision, follow steps of obedience.

- Rebellion: Actively submit to others.

- Lust: Focus on giving value to others.

- Bitterness: Continually release hurts.

- Critical spirit: Value compassion and connection as much as truth.

- Selfish ambition: Surrender to His plan, focus on the good of the whole.

Given the choice, everyone will choose someone else's transforming response. Usually the one that is hardest for a person is the one that is most needed. If it were easy, our good flesh already would have accomplished it. The rebel hates submission, but it is the pathway to transformation for him. The prideful person hates to wait, but it is his salvation. The thing that irritates us the most is generally the very thing that God asks from us.

It is not that God hates us or wants to see us in misery. Actually, it is just that we love our good flesh that much. The thing God is asking from us is to give up our good flesh. We must die to self and make Him Lord. Once we identify our core values and our strongest negative spiritual flows, we can identify what death to self will look like for us.

If we can see the picture from a positive viewpoint, the point of irritation becomes a point of transformation. It is much easier to cooperate with something that we see as a transformation than something we see as simply an irritation. Again, the tool of vision is very, very helpful. And not only that, we can better see that God does love and value us after all. We are not some hopeless monster that God is squishing like a bug. He is allowing these difficulties for the sake of our transformation. Wow! That is a point of understanding that brings life!

Jesus Touches All Who Are Open

A person does have to be open to receiving value. The Pharisees, as a group, were quite full of themselves. The Pharisees saw Jesus as the irritant, and it is very difficult for a person to allow an irritant to be a source of life. Jesus did reach Nicodemus from this group and also Joseph of Arimathea. Some will be open. Some won't. Some will be open one day and not the next. Some will be open continually and will grow much more quickly.

Most of the time, Jesus reached out to those who were down and out. Was it because He loved them more? I don't think so! It was because they were open to connection. In the down and out, the irritations had already done their work. Hope in human strength was waning. The door to connecting was swinging open.

His disciples fit that description. Jesus took a bunch of misfits and turned them into pearls. No, it was not done quickly. At the end of three years, they were still saying and doing some first-class, stupid things. Then came the Holy Spirit. With God's anointing and God's continual presence, the work didn't have to end after three years, but continued for a lifetime.

History tells us that all of the disciples except John (and of course Judas) were martyred for their faith. Not bad for a bunch of misfits.

What was Jesus' method to reach them? He loved them. He walked with them. He gave them vision and things to do. He taught them and corrected them. He did relationship with them. And when He left, He sent the Holy Spirit to continue the work.

Jesus took a bunch of misfits and turned them into pearls.

We all have obstacles, but our greatest obstacle will be the core passion that God has put within us, when it is not fully given to God. Every obstacle is but a pearl waiting to happen. It is an irritation needing the secretion of God's presence. Unfortunately, too much of the time we see ourselves as forsaken by God, a God who doesn't care for us and has no plan for our lives. How far that is from the truth!

God wants to form His image within us, but if the phone line is down, it cannot happen. He wants to use us to help form that image in others, but if our communication is clouded with a critical eye, we are of little use to Him.

Can you see the pearl? Can you see it in yourself? Do you see it coming out of the point of irritation? What about the pearl in others, perhaps in an enemy or an irritant? Maybe that person is a specially placed messenger of God to help transform you!

To be a lifegiver, we must change the way we see life and the way we see people. We must see His glory, even when it is still shrouded by the clothes of the grotesque. When we see Jesus in all things, we allow His presence to turn a grain of sand into the beautiful pearl of the glory of God. That is God's heart for us. May we all learn to embrace it!

> *Jesus, I thank You that we are Your pearl of great price. I thank You that You were willing to die for the church. We mean that much to You. God, help me to never doubt Your heart for me again. Help me to see Your heart for others and to believe and to pray. Amen. (Prayer based on Matthew 13:45–46.)*

Study Guide

1. John 3 tells us that people who are of the darkness love the darkness and hate the light. How is that a problem for those who desire to witness?

2. Luke 6:45 tells us that a person reacts out of the "treasure of the heart." How do we cooperate with how man functions to help turn a person toward being open to the gospel?

3. How did Jesus connect with Nicodemus? How did He connect with the woman at the well? What was the passion of each that Jesus used as a connecting point?

4. Elijah under God's authority did some great things. Describe the good he brought to the kingdom. While running from Jezebel, how does he demonstrate a fleshly picture?

5. List the negative spiritual flows, and describe what each would look like if connected to God. How do both God and man respond to those flows? How do we cooperate to see them transformed?

6. How does a natural pearl form? How does God form His pearl in us?

7. How does God need to change the way you are viewing yourself? What is God's plan for an irritating area? How do you need to change your view of others who are "irritants" to you?

Chapter 11

THE GRACE CANOPY

did it again. I pressed too hard for too long until I hit that stress point of having nothing left to give. Only then did I notice that I was brittle. Only then did I notice that the presence of God had lifted, taken a vacation, and was pushed off to a distance. After reading my writings, which continually focus on staying connected, you may have thought better of me. But, no. With or without understanding, I still am prone to go my own way. I still am prone to slide into the natural resting place of the good flesh.

We all have areas of weakness, and I believe God pushes every one of us to our limit—not to break us, but to keep us weak. When we are weak, we recognize our need to return to Him, to stay connected. (See 2 Corinthians 12:9.) He presses every one of us to a point where we either break, we push Him away and look for our own escape route, or we embrace His grace and go beyond what we ever thought possible in our lives.

God wants much more for us than we would ever think possible, but it is only possible if we stay in Him. (See Ephesians 3:20.) If I don't stay in Him, my burden becomes heavy—too heavy to handle. Strongholds surface. Without Christ, sin rules and reigns. Sure, the average person is able to rearrange some of the furniture and make it look better. Some diets are successful. Some self-help programs do see breakthroughs. But apart from Christ, no one will ever attain the fulness of God's purpose for him. Without Christ, no one will be perfect.

So how do we define perfect? Without sin? Beyond compare in ability? Tell me, which of you reading this book is without sin? Which of you is perfect?

Sin No More

These questions are not unlike Jesus' comments in John 8:7, when He exhorts the crowd who has gathered to accuse the adulterous woman: "He who is without sin among you, let him throw a stone at her first." Notice the phrasing here. It is not "cast the first stone" as we commonly interpret this verse. It is cast the stone at her first, then (I assume) start casting it at everyone else who is guilty, too. Only the perfect One has that right. Only Jesus could cast that stone, and He chooses not to because it would not accomplish His purpose.

In John 8:10–11, we see the conclusion of this incident:

> When Jesus had raised Himself up and saw no one but the woman, He said to her, "Woman, where are those accusers of yours? Has no one condemned you?" She said, "No one, Lord." And Jesus said to her, "Neither do I condemn you; go and sin no more."

I don't know which is more ominous: the question, "Which of you is without sin?" or the statement, "Go and sin no more." If no one in the crowd was without sin, how could Jesus tell a blatant sinner, "Go and sin no more"?

When we go forth to minister, especially to the dysfunctional, we better be able to answer that seeming contradiction, because it will be faced over and over again. On the one hand, we must challenge those to whom we minister to "Go and sin no more." On the other hand, we would do well to advise them that they will surely fail, because as human beings with a fallen nature, they will continue to sin. And how does that ever make sense to anyone?

Perfection

There are actually two different Greek words that are translated as the word *perfect* in multiple instances. Both of these words have as a part of their meaning the idea of becoming complete, or mature. One talks more about the full completion, while the other speaks more of the process of being restored to completeness. These two words give us a different perspective on the biblical concept of perfection, the biblical idea of "Go and sin no more."

In the Scriptures, performance is tied to maturity:

> And that servant who knew his master's will, and did not prepare himself or do according to his will, shall be beaten with many stripes. But he who did not know, yet committed things deserving of stripes, shall be beaten with few. For everyone to whom much is given, from him much will be required; and to whom much has been committed, of him they will ask the more.
>
> —Luke 12:47–48

God does not expect more from us than He has put into us. To whom much is given, much is required. To whom little is given, little is required. There is a reason why God calls us children. We are to be continually dependent on Him. There is a reason why God calls the newly saved person a baby.

The newborn is just starting out on his journey. He has not matured. Little is expected of the newborn. A newborn baby wets his diaper. He cannot eat normal food. Others must feed him. He cannot communicate apart from crying. And we call him perfect—at least the doting parents in the crowd always do.

There are those who only seem to apply the power of the cross to atone for sin for those who are not yet saved. Once a person is saved, he is required to walk in perfection—or confess immediately—or else. I have met many with a theology that would say that having one single unconfessed sin will send you to hell. If the power of the cross extends no farther than that, we all are on shaky ground, indeed. Who among us has been 100 percent accurate in recognizing every single time that he sinned? Who truly has no unconfessed sin?

To place that much value on confession of sin misses the heart of God, the power of the atonement, and a right understanding of sin. Jesus was and is the Son of God. He *died* for us. That is no flimsy atonement. It reaches well beyond those sins that have been legally confessed. It has to, otherwise the newborn babes would have to be immediately mature, immediately perfect with no sin. While the newborn babe in Christ is perfect in many ways, he is not yet spiritually mature and will not be without sin.

Glory of God

How is the newborn babe perfect? Romans 3:23 says, "For all have sinned and fall short of the glory of God." What I find interesting about that verse is that the standard is "the glory of God," and not an attained level of performance. The word *glory* actually has two different connotations that make up its meaning. One is the idea of being weighty or substantial. This concept of the word *glory* actually lines up with a person having godly character, having that spiritual substance laid up in his heart over a period of time. Only mature believers represent this aspect of the word *glory.*

One aspect of glory is walking in His presence . . . the other is growing in maturity.

However, there is another connotation to the word *glory.* That is the idea of a countenance of light and life. Having a spiritual glow. What is amazing, even the newest believer can have this glow. In fact, just like a newborn baby, sometimes the newborns in Christ represent the glow of Christ better than the mature. God's presence is often all over the newly saved, and they can be a better representation of the glory of God than those who are more "sinless."

The definition of the word *sin* is simply "missing the mark." It is not about a list of do's and don'ts, but about walking in a manner that shows forth the glory of God. One aspect of that glory is walking with the glow of His presence covering your whole countenance. The other part is growing in maturity.

Those who try to make sin a works issue might apply a Ten Commandments concept to our theology, and possibly come to a conclusion that most of the time they are walking without sin. The rich young ruler did that. In fact, Jesus even seems to accept his claim that he has obeyed the commandments from his youth, but then raises the standard saying, "If you want to be perfect, go, sell what you have and give to the poor, and you will have treasure in heaven; and come, follow Me" (Matt. 19:21). God's standard is that we measure up to His level of glory, to His level of perfection. Even if the rich young ruler conceivably had obeyed all the Ten Commandments from his youth, he did not measure up to the glory of God, nor to His level of perfection.

Higher Standard

When I apply Jesus' standards, I find something very different from a Ten Commandment, works-type of approach. Jesus said, "But I say to you that whoever looks at a woman to lust for her has already committed adultery with her in his heart" (Matt 5:28). That makes being sinless a little tougher. Jesus defines sin at the heart level. The one who has had anything negative stirred in his heart is already in sin according to Jesus.

Not only that, listen to how these verses in Matthew 5:43–48 up the stakes even more:

> You have heard that it was said, 'You shall love your neighbor and hate your enemy.' But I say to you, love your enemies, bless those who curse you, do good to those who hate you, and pray for those who spitefully use you and persecute you, that you may be sons of your Father in heaven; for He makes His sun rise on the evil and on the good, and sends rain on the just and on the unjust. For if you love those who love you, what reward have you? Do not even the tax collectors do the same? And if you greet your brethren only, what do you do more than others? Do not even the tax collectors do so? Therefore you shall be perfect, just as your Father in heaven is perfect.

There's that word *perfect* again. In the context of the passage it means that we have to love those who hate us and spitefully use us. Ouch. At least in my life, so much for sinlessness. At best, I hope to control my actions and words when someone is ugly to me. But if we combine the two passages, I should never even have so much as a negative heart reaction toward those who spitefully use me. If I do, I am guilty of not loving. If I do, I fall short of the glory of God. If I do, I am not perfect.

Even among the mature saved, who can measure up to this kind of standard? Even including the godliest of all ages, who has ever lived up to the standard of the "glory of God?" Even among the venerated saints, who ever has reached this standard of being perfect?

The correct answer is that every last one of us can live in God's perfection! In God's sight, to whom much is given, much is required. To whom little is given, little is required. And the atonement of Christ is there to cover the person who is making the transition from having little given to him to having much given to him.

The correct answer is that every last one of us can live in God's perfection!

This is where the concepts of spiritual presence and spiritual substance work so well. Once saved, a person is continually capable of manifesting godly spiritual presence. At any point in time, we are capable of staying in humility, staying connected with Christ, and thus manifesting the very presence of Christ despite not being the most mature person spiritually. Godly presence is a kind of immediate covering. We manifest His glory by being vessels of His presence, not by being sinless.

At the same time, as we continually walk in His presence, we are coming to a deeper and deeper level of maturity, where the substance of Christ is increasingly evident in our lives. We have more of His character and wisdom. We are better able to hold up in difficult circumstances. As the years go by, perfect takes on a whole new meaning, a meaning that includes that of a thoroughly tested and tried individual who is consistently walking in godliness. The baby is perfect. So is the mature. But baby behavior is only perfect for the one who is truly a baby.

The Canopy

Baby carriers often have a kind of canopy designed to stretch out over the head of the baby to protect him from the sun or the weather. The grace of God is our canopy, our covering to help cover our imperfections, to keep us in a place of protection as we grow. Yet, picture a thirty- year-old man inside a baby carrier. First of all, the man doesn't fit, and he certainly doesn't fit with the canopy out. No covering is possible for a thirty-year-old baby.

The canopy of grace is more than sufficient to cover all those who are perfect for their age and stage. As we grow and our baby carrier grows into an umbrella, the covering continues to do the job—but not for everyone. In Christ, we have many thirty- and forty-year-old babies. Notice in the following passage how the knowledge of the truth comes before the expectation of judgment:

> For if we sin willfully after we have received the knowledge of the truth, there no longer remains a sacrifice for sins, but a certain fearful expectation of judgment, and fiery indignation which will devour the adversaries.
> —HEBREWS 10:26–27

The one who sins after receiving knowledge is no longer under the canopy of grace. Through knowledge, he has outgrown the baby carrier, yet in lifestyle he can still be stuck in it. When that happens, he can no longer be covered. His level of performance is not matching his level of knowledge, and thus there is an expectation of judgment. With no canopy of grace, he can no longer be described as perfect.

Some take this passage and try to make it a heaven and hell issue. To me, it is more of an issue of being out from under God's covering, out from under the protection that God provides. Those who are "perfect," who are in the range of where they should be at a certain stage of maturity, have the advantage of being under God's covering. Those who rebel, those who refuse to humble themselves, those who continually fail to grow lose the advantage of the covering. They expose themselves to all kinds of trouble. In the end, they probably become bitter and blame God for their troubles.

Levels of Knowledge

While anything that does not measure up to the character and stature of Christ is sin (it misses the mark!), not all sin is the same for all individuals: "Therefore, to him who knows to do good and does not do it, to him it is sin" (James 4:17). Again, the emphasis is on knowledge. The elders and teachers of the church are clearly held to a higher standard. (See James 3:1.) Is it because the standard changed? No way. Christ is the Standard and He never changes. Rather, it is because their level of knowledge is greater. They are more mature. A greater level of godliness is now appropriately required.

This concept is so vital in ministry. With this in mind, "Go and sin no more" takes on a new meaning. This verse is not saying, "Don't ever fail again." More accurately it is saying, "Grow up." Or, "Learn from your mistakes. Don't keep on making the same mistakes over and over." In the instance of the woman caught in adultery, it would be, "Get away from this lifestyle. I have forgiven you once, but now you know better. Learn from Me and grow beyond where you are now."

Many have asked me about the meaning of 1 John 5:16, but it too makes sense in light of what I am sharing:

> If anyone sees his brother sinning a sin which does not lead to death, he will ask, and He will give him life for those who commit sin not leading to death. There is sin leading to death. I do not say that he should pray about that.

Those who are under the canopy of grace, who are at a point of maturity where they do not know any better, simply need an intercessor. Our prayers will cover them and make it as if the sin had never happened. That is the power of the atonement. For those who do know better, who are in willful sin, it is a different story. (Read Hebrews 10.) They have come out from under the covering. Intercession may help turn them back to God, but it cannot erase the effects of the sin, nor move them back under the covering. Only repentance will make a difference for those who are in willful and known sin.

Grace Changes Ministry

Once we accept the theology of the canopy of grace, it totally changes our perspective on ministry. Suddenly we need discernment on what to target in the life of a person and when to target it. As parents, we do not demand maturity of a baby. Yet as believers, we will instantly make a number of demands on a newborn babe in Christ. This is unrealistic and counterproductive.

Seldom can a person grow in more than one area at a time, and while concentrating on a new area, an old baseline can often slip. A person who had made great strides in an area of worry can easily slip back into a worry zone when trying to conquer a new area like lust. He could handle one thing, but the addition of a second challenge seems to make him regress. It can be totally frustrating, but we must learn to work with baselines. As we start to focus on new areas, we must continue to reinforce old areas lest they rise up again.

By then we realize that the bar is moving and that the real standard is Christ.

As we grow, God continues to move the bar. He sets it a little bit higher. The more mature we get, the more we realize how far we still have to go. By then we realize that the bar is moving and that the real standard is Christ. Mature? "Yes!" Perfect? "Yes!" Sinless? "No!" We may be hitting the mark for our maturity level, but none of us measures up to the glory of God—except through the presence. And that is a gift.

As I said, God keeps us weak. Dependent. Connected. And flowing in His presence—if we throw out our works theology and grab onto a connected and receiving theology. Instead, some try to hang on to an Old Testament theology of sin. They read the Ten Commandments and like the rich young ruler, declare, "I am without sin." If it is spiritual substance they are seeing, if it is the heart they are seeing, how could they ever make such a statement? Only those who focus on the outward man and ignore the stuff of the heart would ever be so foolish as to think of themselves as being without sin.

The rest of us choose to accept the canopy of grace and to rest in that covering. No, it is not a rest that is presumptuous. We know that tomorrow more will be required. We know we must grow. The canopy moves even as the cloud moved in the desert for the Israelites. We must not be left behind. We don't have a cloud by day and a pillar of fire by night like the Israelites did, but the canopy is real and a very present help. It is a resting point. We are truly perfect while under the canopy.

Failing Forward

With this understanding, failure takes on such a completely new perspective. Our goal should be to *fail forward*. Surely our weaknesses will manifest. God will allow them to surface or even test us to a point where they do come forth. If we are never tested, we never see it or confess it, nor do we grow. God provokes, even knowing that we will fail, but hoping that when we fail, we will turn to Him. If we turn to Him, we will fail forward. We will recognize our weakness, connect with Him, and be strengthened through our failure. We will receive His substance and presence in the very place of our weakness and be strengthened at our point of need. When this happens, we have a great chance of failing forward and of making our fall a stepping-stone to success.

Times of testing take on a new perspective when we realize what God is doing through the test. A test is actually a vote of confidence from God. He expects us at the very least to fail forward, or better yet to catch ourselves before the point of outward failure. If we can catch it at a heart level, we can repent and grow without having to sow the bad seed, without having to set the bad example, and then recover from the bad fruit later on. That is true wisdom. That is the ultimate for the man of God. The test brings the twinge of heart, which is immediately seen and recognized and stopped before it ever comes forth. It can happen!

Failure is never fatal unless it is final.

With this model, people look different. Discerning eyes are much more possible. We can believe—yes, see—God's purpose even when failure is right in front of us. We can still have faith! Failure is never fatal unless it is final. When the person who refuses to get up, gives up, then failure takes them into defeat. Otherwise, failure is but a stepping-stone to take us back to the presence of God. How can that mean anything but victory? Unfortunately, too many people do not see it that way. Rather, they choose to continue to beat themselves up and to hope that feeling bad will bring a change. But it won't. Only connecting with God will bring the change.

Some would fear that this model takes sin and failure too lightly. It doesn't. It demands that the person with knowledge grow. But all growth comes from being connected and not from better performance. Better performance is nothing but good flesh. I suggest that most of those who would say the model is taking sin too lightly are actually placing more of a premium on performance than they are the flow of grace that comes through being connected.

The Power of Grace

It is the connection with God that empowers us to live godly. The word *grace* has two meanings. Grace is closely associated with forgiveness. That is the canopy, the covering of forgiveness we have been talking about. But grace also means empowering. Because we are under the covering of forgiveness, we also can connect and become empowered to live right. The grace canopy both covers and connects.

When we understand the grace canopy, ministry becomes much more about timing and growth. We can't expect instant maturity. Thus, we must see an individual's greatest need. Usually the love and acceptance of Christ is one of the first baselines, but it is different for each individual. A child learns to crawl and then walk. Newborn believers begin by learning to love and be loved. They continue in their training by learning patience and faithfulness. It is one baseline after another. In most cases, we need to focus more on these positives than we do on getting rid of the bad habits.

Often there are some major bad habits that the Lord will, as a gift, dissolve away from the person. Sometimes the bad habits are a significant hindering force and need to go for the sake of the next baseline. Sometimes the bad habits will not go until there is good fruit from the next baseline. A person who is a worrier may use smoking as a crutch to physically mask some of the fear. This kind of smoker will find it much easier to quit after he begins to deal with the spirit of fear. In other cases, the smoking is more of an "in your face" rebellion to God. This person will need to humble himself and move toward quitting as an active part of crushing the rebellious heart. Sometimes habits are more of a symptom. Sometimes they are more bound up with the very core of the spiritual growth.

God's Cheerleaders

The lifegiver learns to see what God is doing in the life of an individual and then cooperates with that work. There is a canopy of grace. It doesn't all have to be fixed at once. Something that is irritating to me may not be the highest priority to God. We need to look for the spiritual flows that God is establishing in the person and then reinforce those flows.

We cannot make a person perfect nor mature. We can only be an influence. We can see what God is doing and become a cheerleader. We can do our best to connect to God and to impart some godly substance to an individual to help him with his growth. We can see what God is doing and have faith. We can pray and intercede at the points of difficulty. We can expect them to fail forward. We can believe them from glory to glory; from victory to victory; from perfection to perfection. Or maybe, from failure to connectedness to growth—is that more realistic?

Not necessarily from God's point of view. He is like a Father doting over a newborn child. He doesn't see the immaturity—only the perfection. He is the One who describes us as moving from glory to glory. (See 2 Corinthians 3:18.) And because of the grace canopy, God does not have rose-colored glasses. He will see people through to their potential and their created purpose.

Even so, as we mature, we do see the bar move. We fail again and again, hopefully which leads to greater dependence. God keeps even the mature on that edge of failure by adding burdens of intercession for others, and levels of spiritual warfare that will test the spiritual muscle of even the strong. Why? To keep us at a point of dependence (which is the place of growth!).

Yes, even today I struggle. But that's a good thing. I am under the canopy of grace. I am perfect—but not, actually. I am a sinner and yet a saint; a failure, and yet moving toward success. I slide into that negative, load-bearing person, get heavy, and then get connected. I'd really like to be perfectly on top of things all the time, but I find myself struggling—or growing again after I reconnect. The grace canopy is our hope. It is the source of our ability to believe for others. Even when we struggle, and even when they struggle. Especially when we struggle, it is our hope.

> *My God and my Father, I realize that the place from which You see our lives is very different from my self-absorbed daily living. With my limited vision, I struggle to find my way in life. God, give me Your perspective and keep me reminded that the most important thing in life is to become more like You. Amen. (Prayer based on Romans 8:28–29.)*

Study Guide

1. Why does God allow us (or even press us) to get to the breaking point spiritually? What are God's purposes in allowing us to be pressured?

2. How can we in good conscience tell someone to, "Go and sin no more"? What do you think Jesus meant by this statement when He said it to the woman caught in adultery?

3. How is the newborn babe in Christ perfect? What is needed for the new Christian to continue to walk in biblical perfection?

4. If perfection is partially about age and stage, how can we know where a person should be at any given point in time? On what basis do we give them guidance on needed areas of growth?

5. Failure takes on a whole new meaning within a grace theology. How does failure work to actually lead a person toward growth in Christ? When does it lead to a negative end?

6. What are some baselines that a child goes through in developmental stages? What are some baselines that a Christian must go through on his path toward maturity?

7. Where in your life have you struggled with a sense of failure? What is God trying to do in this area of your life? Is it a baseline needing work, or a gifting out of balance? How does this chapter change your perspective?

Chapter 12

FOLLOWING THE VOICE

Most ministry models will have some kind of "how to" list. So here's the list: follow the voice of God. That's it. I'm sure it's a disappointment to some of you, but that's it. The reality is that we are dealing with people. No two persons are alike. No one responds the same. There are definitely principles to see and to understand. That helps. But ultimately it comes down to following the voice of God.

Just take the last chapter as an illustration of my point. If I accept a theology that includes the canopy of grace, as a lifegiver I have to decide when to confront an issue and when to wait until a more appropriate time to deal with the issue. If the grace of God truly does cover some of the more hidden sins of the immature and for that matter even the more mature, when is it time to drag those things out into the open and make an issue of them? When should I keep my mouth shut? There is no formula that will provide you the answer. Follow the voice of God.

The Problem

Now the real problem: I find very few people today who are comfortable with their ability to hear the voice of God. Nor are they comfortable depending on divine direction for decisions that critically affect their future. That is a problem!

Once again, having a worldview that actively incorporates the idea of spiritual function and spiritual flow makes a huge difference. Since the sixteenth century, the Western church has been drifting more and more toward a rationalistic approach to Christianity. This means that people expect God to communicate through the thought mode. They expect a thought to come into their heads, and to be able to think their way to a clear understanding of what God is saying.

Without a doubt, we must come to a conscious understanding of what God is speaking, but the "voice" of God more often begins at the spirit level and not at the thought level. Even when there are God planted thoughts, we still have to discern between what is God and what is not. I said, *discern*; this is not a rational exercise. Logic can lead a person anywhere he wants to go by just slightly changing the premise. Logic is not a basis for discernment. True spiritual discernment will be a "sense" of what is right and what is not.

Logic is not a basis for discernment.

Again, there is another difficulty. Our spiritual senses tend to be shaped by our spiritual past. The person who is used to a yelling and screaming environment, actually will feel more comfortable in a great deal of vibrant activity, even if it is negative in tone. If God were to call that person to sit and wait quietly before Him, he would be crawling on the inside within a few minutes. His spiritual antenna, his "discernment," would tell him that he had missed God. Our spiritual antennae tend to line up with our spiritual past and not with what is right.

Discerning God's Will

So how do we begin to discern between what is something that is merely a product of our spiritual past and what is truly God? The normal state of fallen man is good flesh. We do our best to move into a place where we can feel good about self, doing good works and thinking good thoughts. As long as our lives are tolerable and we do not slip off into too many negative behaviors, we will likely stay in the good flesh zone. While in this zone, we are actually resisting the voice of God, and embracing the behavior patterns of the past. Then comes a crisis (or several of them) and the negative substance comes to the surface in a way so that it is obvious that it is negative. As discussed earlier, good flesh is actually a negative spiritual flow. It just doesn't look like it. It is a person depending on self instead of getting connected into God. Living in a self-centered state is sin. Any crisis exposes the good flesh for what it is. It is an independent, living for self, life.

The person who is living in good flesh while not in crisis can easily come to the Scriptures and begin to integrate biblical content into his thinking. This further confuses the picture. He thinks that he is following the will of God because he is integrating the concepts of God into his thinking. But the will of God cannot be done until we connect with God, forsake our selfishness, and serve Him. We prefer to be good people and to feel good about ourselves. We prefer to think good thoughts and to do good works. A crisis in our lives will expose the weakness of this approach.

There is a difference between good thoughts and God thoughts, between good works and God works. The key difference is in connectedness and in substance. The source for good works is self. The source for God works is God. If I am depending on self, I can do good works and think good thoughts, but I am still basically egocentric. I am serving self. Only when I truly move from selfishness to humility can I move from the good to the godly. To tell the difference requires discernment (spiritually given!), or a crisis. At the point of crisis, a breakdown in behavior exposes the true inner substance that is operating. When the inner substance shows up in outward actions, I call that fruit. It is the true heart motive coming out in clear ways.

Follow the Fruit

To get an accurate picture of life, we must learn to follow the fruit, to pay attention to the flows of the heart, and to discern the presence that is operating. It is not difficult to discern the difference between the very wicked and the very good. That is easy. At least for most it is easy. In today's world, what is godly is beginning to be accepted by some as being wicked. Those who try to share the love of Christ with others are seen as evil in today's culture. They are called intolerant and described as bigots. Many people are significantly influenced by this cultural bias, and actually feel a sense of shame when they try to share the gospel. For those who do feel this shame, their spiritual senses have been warped by a culture that is out of line with God's Word.

Once we realize that the conscience is shaped by the spiritual past, this is not surprising. Some people have grown up with a spiritual past that says spiritual things are private and should not be shared with others. Those who have this spiritual background will feel violated by a public testimony of the gospel. They will feel like it is wrong. When the spiritual foundations are wrong, the spiritual discernment will be wrong and the logic will come alongside to support the ego to create a united front. The person is at "peace" with himself, but he is wrong according to the Word of God.

All of us have some wrong foundations and thus the potential for wrong spiritual judgments and wrong thoughts with respect to good and evil. Where there are wrong foundations, even seemingly obvious choices between good and evil will become confusing. I can remember during my college years rolling over in my mind whether or not it was OK spiritually for a man and a woman to live together without being married. I reasoned that as long as they were faithful to each other, how could it hurt?

Despite my upbringing, despite being in a Bible study at the time, I remember thinking those thoughts. Clearly they do not line up with Scripture, but my logical mind was playing with those thoughts trying to make sense of them and *to discern why it could be wrong.* I was being influenced by some of the thinking of the sexual revolution. Because of the biblical influence, it was not likely that I would have fully given over to it. But for a time, I was trying to give that thinking some space. I wanted to feel more a part of and in touch with those around me. I wanted to feel good about me, and about my good flesh.

Logic can lead a person anywhere. I was quickly becoming a product of my college environment and of the modern culture and I didn't even know it. As is typical, I was seeking some kind of religious cover for my thoughts in the Scriptures, and with a few logical gymnastics I was at least having enough success to ponder it for a time.

Follow the Word

Looking back, I can't believe I even wasted my time thinking about it. The Word is absolutely clear on this subject. This is one of the first principles in following the voice of God: when it is clear in the Word, don't even think about playing the logic games. Humble yourself and obey.

Humble yourself. That sounds like a spiritual substance kind of term. Compare that with my vain intellectual ponderings about a man and a woman living together. In retrospect, I can check out the spiritual substance of the two and it is obvious which is of God. In my ponderings, I had made myself a god, trying to discern what was best for society, thinking about the potential outcomes. That was vanity. Not surprisingly, my thought life was wrong. Fortunately, it never went past a time of pondering. I learned to humble myself in that area to the clear teaching of the Word.

> *God speaks to the humble, but for the proud there is nothing but silence.*

So much of life is covered by clear commandments and principles in the Word of God. When we commit our entire being toward following these teachings, we have a great start toward following the voice of God. It gives guidelines to our thinking, to our actions, and it causes us to walk in a spirit of humility. As humility begins to be worked into our spiritual fabric, we are a long ways toward being able to connect with the voice of God. God speaks to the humble, but for the proud there is nothing but silence, a silence that will be filled with vain, egoistic ramblings.

For some, these ramblings use the content of Scripture, and so they feel justified. For those who learn to discern between pride and humility, vanity is vanity, whether it includes Scripture in its thinking or not. The first principle of hearing the voice of God is not being able to quote scriptural things so much as it is beginning to obey scriptural commands.

However, we can't stop there. Life cannot be reduced to a set of principles and commandments to be followed. Life is far too complex and people are too unique for us to have a set of rules to guide us in all things. We must be in active contact with almighty God for further advice. It seems most Christians in our nation talk about having heard the voice of God only a few times in their lives if even that. This should not be.

Spiritual Communion

God sent His Holy Spirit to be with us and to commune with us on a constant basis. That does not sound like a God who wants us to hear from Him once a year or once every few years. The problem is that we are listening for the wrong thing. We are listening for thoughts. God's primary communication is spiritual, though the spiritual must impact the conscious realm for it to be effective and understood. In a culture that has exalted rationalism, we expect everything to come through the mind. The mind is involved, but the Holy Spirit communes first and foremost with our spirits, not our minds.

What does that mean? It means that we must develop our spiritual perception, our spiritual seeing and hearing. It means that He will impact spiritual presence and spiritual substance, which will then overflow into a change in thoughts. When we become attentive to spiritual things, we will begin to "hear" the voice of the Spirit.

We live in a world where almost all of our conscious attention is focused on our thoughts and feelings. The key to hearing the Spirit is to begin to focus more of our conscious attention on our spiritual part. Much of this book has already taught how to be attentive to our spiritual part. When we do learn to be more attentive to spirit and spiritual flows, our thought life more easily can be brought into submission to Christ.

Spirit and Mind

The spirit and the mind are like two train tracks running side by side. There can be crossovers or points where the two merge into one track for a time. Generally both are headed in the same direction, and one gives a clue to the location of the other, but the two tracks are still capable of having two sets of trains running on them.

I see this especially when people are trying to find the will of God for their lives. Often, their minds are going one hundred miles per hour trying to come up with some kind of solution to the problem. The irony is that the more intent a person gets on finding the will of God, the less likely that person is actually going to step into the center of that will. Why? Because we have been trained primarily to pay attention to the mind and the emotions. We ignore the flow of the Spirit.

The spirit and the mind are like two train tracks running side by side.

The person who is in hyper mode has a clear flow of the spirit. It could be described as anxiety or being self-absorbed or just pressing. None of those terms denotes a positive spiritual flow. Where the parallel train track is going, it is almost assured that the second set of tracks is moving in a similar direction.

I visited with a pastor of a church that was considering selling some land to a restaurant that served alcohol. The restaurant had made an offer that the church could hardly refuse. It would launch them into their building process in a major way. The pastor reasoned that the restaurant was not a bar. It was a restaurant that served alcohol. He and others would go to that restaurant if it were there. It seemed hypocritical to consider anything other than going forward. All the logic was running in one direction.

The pastor then consulted some godly men that he knew who challenged this pastor saying that to go forward might be a compromise. They gave him several examples of ministries that had backed away from questionable dealings, and then had seen the blessing of God despite what "good sense" might have indicated was the right decision. Now the pastor had two logical tracks going, with no decision in sight.

In the middle of the night, not able to sleep, the pastor finally surrendered to the second option. When I spoke with him, he was still wondering if he had done the right thing. As I described to him the spirit and soul parallels, it was as if a lightbulb went on. In retrospect, he could clearly see that the entire time he was considering option one, his spiritual flow was in a human enterprising, pressing flow. It was not in a connected, godly flow. As soon as he made the decision to separate from anything questionable, there was a complete spiritual release and a sense of connectedness to God. Bingo! He had hit pay dirt. He had found the will of God, not because of logic, but through the influence of the Spirit of God upon his spirit.

That is a great example of what I am talking about. When we are considering something like the will of God, all we are seeing or hearing is the activity of the soul. It is very easy for our thoughts and feelings to play games with us (the heart is deceitful above all things!).

Instead, we need to learn to pay more attention to our spiritual flow. If we are uptight and pressing, if we are caught up in a human accomplishment flow, it is certain that we are not connected with God. If we are not connected, we are not in the will of God. That does not mean that the decision is wrong, just that it is being pursued in the wrong way. It is possible to make the right decision and still be fearful about that decision. It is possible to make the wrong decision and be fearful about it. It is possible to make the wrong decision and feel good about it, if that decision fits the person's spiritual past that is built on a wrong foundation. Again, we must lay God's foundation in our lives before our discernment becomes consistently reliable.

The Umpire

For many, it will be a real change in seeking the will of God by starting at the point of getting connected with God and continually paying attention to the spiritual flow. As long as I am connected to God, I have a spiritual barometer. Colossians 3:15 says, "And let the peace of God rule in your hearts, to which also you were called in one body; and be thankful." The peace of God should "rule" in our hearts. One translation says the peace of God should be the "umpire" (AMP).

If we are continually connected to God, we learn the spiritual feel of God's peace. It becomes our norm. When it comes time to make a decision, the umpire of God's peace is very real to us. We can tell the difference between human peace and God's peace. For those who are not regularly connected to God, using the umpire of God's peace is at best a guessing game. If we don't regularly walk with God, why would we suddenly expect to be able to walk with Him when we need to make a decision?

Those who learn well the feel of God's peace are able to put their decisions to the test of God's umpire. In matters not clearly guided by the Word of God, the peace of God should be a significant aide in making the final call on whether or not something is the will of God.

Getting Additional Help

In my experience, I have found that I tend to get on a good flesh roll more often than I realize. The peace of God is not adequate in itself, because I can be simply trusting in self more than God. I need godly authority figures in my life to give me another perspective, persons who will hopefully know me well enough to know when I am connected to God and when I am not. Like the pastor described above, all the logic was flowing in one direction. He could begin to taste success as a pastor. A new building. More people. Glitz and glamour. Of course, more souls won to Christ and God getting the glory. Then he spoke with a trusted counselor.

In the end, the umpire of the Spirit made the call, but not without the help of a trusted friend. I get suspicious of anyone who is not willing to submit to a number of tests. Very seldom does God call a person to go it alone. If key authority figures are speaking against a decision, most of the time it is good, at the very least, to stop and reevaluate. Usually it means, "Don't go there!"

A final aide in determining the will of God is circumstances. Too many people use circumstances to guide their way. When this happens, it is more like fatalism: "I was lonely; this girl showed up and spoke to me; it must be God—she is the one for me." How crazy can it get? I've been told stories like that in my marriage counseling!

Circumstances should only be used as a final confirmation. It is appropriate, at times, to say, "God, if this is not where You want me to go, close the door." Sometimes, people say this out of laziness. They don't do the work of discerning what the Spirit is speaking, and again, it becomes a life guided by "whatever" happens, and not by the will of God. Sometimes, if a door is not opening, we need to pray it open. Again, how can we know that unless we are hearing the voice of God?

Circumstances should only be used as a final confirmation.

Even if I choose to surrender my decisions to trusted friends, I use circumstances as a final check, but only as a final check. Once I have done the work to seek Him out, God does confirm His will some way in the natural realm. Sometimes it is through a person's speaking to me. Sometimes it is through money being provided for the project. Sometimes it is a door opening, or closing. God can close a door that no man can open. If we are not being lazy, we need to claim that as a promise, after we have legitimately sought His voice!

When I am searching out the voice of God, I am continually aware of my ability to go off on a self-tangent and still believe that it is God. This happens at the thinking level. It also happens at the spiritual level. Recall the pastor described above; there were two sets of logic. Both seemed to be of God. There were two spiritual flows. One was of God and one was not, but even in our testing of spiritual flows we can be deceived. The spiritual flow was easier to identify than the logic, but only after he consulted with other godly men.

We need to become much more aware of and attentive to spiritual flow. If the flow is wrong, we are not where we need to be yet. It still might be the right decision, but it is not being done in the right way, or it may not be the right time yet. Sometimes a lack of peace just means "Not yet!"

When I learn to rest in God, I can trust what is happening in my mind to a much greater degree. The spirit and the soul tend to be parallel train tracks. If I am spiritually connected, my spiritual part will stimulate a godly flow in the area of imagination and thoughts. That has been my experience as I minister to people. When I press, I have little to give. Occasionally it is good logic. It might even be the right solution—but it lacks life.

Do you need a rule for ministry? Connect with God and follow the flow. Everything else is just rules and lacks the power of God to bring real change. So relax, rest, connect, and follow the One who is the true Lifegiver.

> *Father God, teach me to quiet my mind so that I can connect with You and drink of Your life. Lord, I know that You will help me interpret the work of Your Spirit in me and that You will confirm what You speak through Your Word. I also know that You want to speak to me more than I want to hear. Teach me to rest in You and I will thank You and praise You always. Amen. (Prayer based on 1 Corinthians 14:15; Ephesians 5:17-21.)*

Study Guide

1. Hearing the voice of God begins with learning to be attentive to spiritual flow. Having read this chapter, what does that mean to you?

2. Describe an event from your life where spirit, soul, and body were on parallel tracks. Show how the actions, thoughts, and spiritual flow all lined up.

3. What role does the Word of God and obedience to the Word play in hearing the voice of God? What happens if I bypass the Word?

4. Have there been times for you when the logic of two sides of a decision seemed equally split? How did you ultimately make that decision? What role did the Spirit's influence play in that decision? In light of this chapter, would you have approached the situation differently?

5. For the pastor in the chapter, what role did a godly authority figure play in his decision? What role should authority figures play in our decisions?

6. How do people often use circumstances to determine the will of God? What is the appropriate role for circumstances in determining the will of God?

7. Think of a recent decision or even a current decision that may be pending. Did you take (or are you taking) the time to get connected before trying to discern the will of God? What are the spiritual flows surrounding that decision? How can those flows give you a better sense of the will of God?

Chapter 13

WEIGHTING FOR GOD

When I first started as a pastor, the weight of the ministry was staggering to me. It should not have been that way. God was there to enable me, but I chose to shoulder the load in my human strength on a continual basis. Walking mostly alone, the ministry was heavy.

As I started catching on to this concept of getting connected and staying connected, I began to deal with my heaviness by retreating to times of prayer. It often took me hours (and in a few cases even days!) to release the human load that I was carrying. At the time, I didn't realize that it was pride that was making the load heavy and that it was also pride that so drastically slowed down my ability to get connected with God. I was much better at *weighting* for God than at *waiting* for God.

Because of my pride, I thought that I had the ability to carry the load. One of my greatest needs was to fail while operating at this human level, so that I would be brought to a point of humility and dependence. I was in agony because I thought I had to get it right. The more I pressed, the heavier the load became until it would get to the point of agony. When we walk in pride, our level of pain is multiplied significantly beyond what it would have been otherwise. Typically, we then blame God for the incredible pain we are experiencing.

Time and again, I came to that place of prayer. Time and again, I left connected. Time and again, I lost it as soon as I stepped back into a good flesh life, trusting once again in my human abilities. My life consisted of prayer retreats and passionate pursuit of God—or so

I thought. Actually, there was a whole lot more good flesh going on during my "passionate pursuit" than I realized.

Not until God began to purge the pride did I see a significant change in this pattern. I am finally learning to live more connected. The heaviness is not necessary. If I am heavy, I can almost guarantee that I have slipped into pride and am not connected. I am not a life-giver. I am not connected to the flow or the voice.

I went through the same process in counseling and ministry. We tend to be spiritually consistent in all we do. I was heavy at home, heavy in ministry, and heavy in counseling. There was spiritual consistency. I depended way too much on self. What we are doing spiritually in one area, we are usually doing in another area. If not, we are likely psychotic.

In counseling, I would do my best to use good listening technique. I thought hard. I counseled with intensity. I prayed with fervency. There are just too many I's in that list. And I felt it. I carried it heavy. God was teaching and shaping my thought life during that time. I often had good advice because of what I was learning, but I saw minimal positive results because the pride limited my ability to connect with God.

My advice has changed little through the years—but my ministry has changed drastically. I had mostly biblical thoughts twenty years ago, but at that time, I depended on my thoughts. Today, I am learning to depend on the flow of the Spirit. He is much more effective than anything I can do or say. What a difference!

My ministry today is not nearly so dependent on me. I try to be attentive to and to wait upon the flow of the Spirit. If there is nothing there, I am learning that I have nothing to give and so I wait. When I have nothing clear from the Lord, I ask questions or I say, "Let's pray." Then we wait and listen. If there is still nothing, I don't try to prove how much I don't know. At least I try to keep my mouth shut and hope that God will reveal something before the next time around.

Compassion

As I stated in the last chapter, we must start our pursuit of God's voice by coming under the authority of the clearly revealed commandments. We need to read and study the Word to establish a good spiritual baseline of operation. We continue to grow in recognizing His voice by establishing godly authorities in our lives. We all have a tendency to follow our own hearts, and we have only a limited ability to see where we leave off and where God begins. We need others to help keep us in check.

This foundation must be in place before going on to the more subjective "hearing" of the voice of God that I will be describing. Unless a person has laid the biblical foundations of the Word and of obedience, any "sensing" of God's voice will be nothing more than a person following after the whims of his own heart. Even as the sin nature has created in us a pull toward good flesh, even so the sin nature will try to make us think that our thoughts are God's thoughts. Only when we are being renewed by the Holy Spirit and are growing in godly foundations will we get to a point where we can reliably discern between God's voice and our voice.

However, the biblical foundations and applications of God's principles do not replace the need to grow in spiritual sensitivity. The general application of the Word is helpful but does not supply the dynamic of the immediate touch of the Holy Spirit. The immediate touch of God is a powerful tool to help people move to a point of victory. The Holy Spirit is more than ready to come along side our spirit and bring an influence that is His voice. He moves us to a point of thankfulness or praise. He convicts us of sin or commends us for deeds well done.

All of this is done beyond the normal flow of our thought lives. Obviously, we must learn to fix our eyes on what the Spirit is doing and become consciously aware of it in order to cooperate with it. When we focus on what is happening in our spiritual flows, it does hit our thought lives. But it doesn't originate there. We observe it. We take note of what the Spirit is doing in us, and then we interpret the moving of the Spirit and we respond to it.

In the same way, the Spirit speaks to us in ministry by influencing our spirit to understand what another person is experiencing. For me, I sense an overlay over my own spirit of what the other person is feeling. Sometimes I can "see" it on the person's face. It is hard to describe, but there is a compassion connection, which is the voice of God. Having taken note of what I sense the Spirit doing within me, I then share what God is "speaking" with the other person.

As long as there is godly compassion, we can be confident that God is directing the process through His Spirit quickening our spirit in the direction that He wants us to move. I don't need logic at that point. I need sensitivity to the spiritual flow. Where He is flowing, He is leading. It is His voice. It is my job to simply share with the other person what I am sensing. It may be loneliness within him, or perhaps frustration. Sometimes it is anger or in other instances it is confusion.

This doesn't seem like ministry to us. We want to give principles from God's Word or we want to give solutions. God wants to demonstrate to the hurting that He understands what the person is going through and that He desires to connect with the person. Again, we tend to live in an action or thinking realm and God lives much more in a connecting realm. Connecting is ministry and will produce a far greater result than our own vain efforts.

That does not mean that God won't deal with the person's thought life or behaviors. Later in the process, God often brings to mind Scriptures that will deal with these areas. However, most of the time there is an order in ministry. I find that God generally connects before He rebukes. We have taught that the rebuke comes first, then the repentance, then the connection. In most cases, I find that connection is needed to prepare the person to receive the conviction.

> *Connecting is ministry and will produce a far greater result than our own vain efforts.*

As long as there is compassion connecting me to what the other person is experiencing, I stay in that mode and spend time identifying with the person. I identify by describing what I am sensing, letting the person know that God knows what is happening in his heart. There is so much more happening during these times than we can ever account for intellectually.

Again, it is very easy for a person in ministry to lose connectedness with God during this process and to take off in a way that is being dictated by his own heart or feelings. To prevent this, I try to do some continual reality checks. Does the other person seem to be on the same page with me? Are there appropriate responses in the person (like tears or smiles) at appropriate times that let me know that I really am connected and not just on a chase of my own?

To discern this, it is helpful for us to keep our eyes open while ministering to a person. For some, having eyes open distracts them from sensing what God is speaking. To minister well, we need to develop the ability of focus on God, even with the distraction of physical sight. It is helpful to physically see what is happening in order to check it with what we are spiritually sensing. In some cases, the person can be playing a game with us and what is happening on the face is a lie. In most cases, that game will be evident on the face of the person, even as true ministry will also be evident.

It is also very good to openly ask the person if what we are sensing is truly describing what is happening within him. If the person says we are missing the mark, it is time to stop. Either we really are missing the mark, or the person is being touched but is not ready to deal with it right now. Either way, we should not press forward without an active connection *and* cooperation.

If the connectedness to the other person suddenly stops (and there is not some human reason for the shutdown), I assume that the interruption is an indication of the voice of God. Many times when the flow has come to an abrupt stop, I have spoken something like, "You don't feel like God could ever love you." Time and again when the flow is interrupted, the words just spoken have been effective at identifying a blockage that needs to be dealt with.

Often I sense that the connection has stopped, and I feel it as a cold, disconnectedness in my own spirit. Usually people are not bold enough to tell me that the connection has stopped, and I have found that it is helpful at these times to say to them, "I am sensing that God seems very distant to you and that you are struggling with feeling connected to Him."

We should not press forward without an active connection and cooperation.

When the person is in a disconnected state and I identify it for the person, it is like a wave of relief comes over the person. People seem to internalize that the disconnectedness is their own fault, and they see it as evidence that they will never get any better. To let them know that God has the situation under control, and that the blockage is now at least partially identified, is usually a great relief to the person.

Over the years I've learned not to trust my logic. Despite all my training and years of counseling, prayer is continually more effective at identifying and healing bondages than any of the ideas I get while talking with the person. Talking with the person does provide a human point of connection and is helpful, but it seldom heals any root issues.

As I've learned to connect with God's Spirit, spiritual flow has been the key to finding areas that need ministry and prayer provides the touch that brings the healing and victory. The insights from my counseling are weak comparatively and in most cases need to be applied after the Spirit has spoken instead of before we hear from God. The touch of God's current presence and voice are the key.

Again, I do want to reiterate a disclaimer. A person can be deceived by spiritual flow just as easily as he can be deceived by his own thought life. It is always good to have an overview of all that is happening, checking it against the Word of God and the clear principles that are found in the Word. Whether it is a thought or a spiritual flow, if it is contrary to the Word of God, it is wrong. As human beings, we are capable of being attentive to multiple things at one time. We can be attentive to spiritual flow and still have a backdrop of comparison with the principles of the Word.

Learning to follow the voice of God by sensing spiritual flows is a skill to be learned. It is trial and error. No one will excel at it overnight. Hebrews 5:14 tells us that we become mature in this "solid food" by exercising our spiritual senses over and over again. We must come to an understanding of what is God and what is just our own thinking in order for us to be effective in ministry.

When I learn to be sensitive to what is happening in my spiritual flow and to be sensitive to others spiritually, I am much more capable of hearing the voice of God in a ministry context. For most people, what is happening at the spirit level is operating subconsciously. It is an unknown. They have even less awareness of the spirit-to-spirit interplay that is happening between two persons.

We are spiritual beings. Whenever we are in the presence of another person, there is a spiritual interplay. When we are in the presence of demons or angels there is a similar spiritual interplay. Most people in our culture are completely unaware of the spiritual realm and as such are pawns of arguments. For them, hearing the voice of God is a game of guessing which thought pattern is the voice of God. Some try to logically apply the Word, but that too is inadequate in many situations. Being sensitive to the Spirit's voice is a better way. It is the umpire of the spirit that will ultimately give us the minute-by-minute guidance that we need for life and ministry.

Waiting for Connection

For me, one of the easiest ways to lose my connection to the Spirit is when I start taking my role too seriously. When I understand that I am just an influence (and not God!), I tend to relax and get connected. That is part of why it used to take me so long to get connected. I would "press in" to God. The pressing prevented the connection. Not till I got too tired to press did I finally connect!

My approach now is so different from what it used to be. As I am listening to a person, I am also attentive to the person's spiritual flow and to what I am sensing that the Spirit is speaking to me. Sometimes I will sense a high level of connection to the person. When this kind of compassion is present, I generally take that as an indication that

God is at work, though it is important to note that there is a human level of compassion, which can become compulsive and driving. One type of compassion is of God and one is not. Spiritual discernment is needed to tell the difference.

When we have moved into compulsion, we have moved out of God. It is time to go back to prayer and to connect. We are not capable of ministry when we have been overtaken by the compulsive flow that is actually our good flesh. Ministry to others is about connecting with and staying in the flow of the Spirit. Period. That is His voice. That is the manner in which He releases His power.

Sometimes our thoughts will be enlightened during a ministry time and sometimes they won't. The two train tracks (of spirit and mind) don't necessarily intersect. They are parallel. There are times when a spiritual flow brings a clear line of thinking. There are times when there is nothing in thought or feeling. Those are times to wait. We cannot run ahead of Him. Thoughts are not necessary. Waiting is.

What great training waiting is to minister to others. When we learn to still our minds and wait upon God, we will be able to wait for that connecting point with others. We no longer have to be in a hurry to run ahead and fix the problem. We recognize that we cannot fix the problem anyway. Only the Spirit of God can fix anything. Getting that person connected to God on a continual basis is the ultimate solution.

Fixing *a* problem is not fixing *the* problem. Every problem we have is symptomatic of not being under the authority of God and in the will of God. As counselors, we can fix a whole bunch of problems and never offer the true help that is needed. Every person needs God in the here and now, and for all time. Most church people simply want to get people to pray a salvation prayer or perhaps fix an immediate situation. True salvation connects people to God with a connection that continues and is strengthened for all eternity.

Because we have pursued God from a primarily intellectual and works model, we have not understood the concept of being continually connected, nor continually guided. The umpire of spiritual flow should be a constant check for us as to whether we are being guided by the Spirit or not.

If I become brittle, I am not in godly flow. I am likely in good flesh. If I enter into a rigid judgment of another, and that person becomes a lesser person to me, I am not connected. If my lust stirs me up with fantasies of "taking" another person, I am not flowing in God. We have learned to suppress thoughts of lust or unforgiveness. We have not learned how to connect with God and to be renewed in the "spirit" of our minds (Eph. 4:23).

Having the Right Focus

The power of the atonement truly sets us free. God does not have to mature a person instantly. He actually can tolerate some areas of sin in our lives until we have had time to grow, until we get to a point where we are now ready and able to put off those immaturities. The death of Christ is effective. It covers sin. It gives God the option of waiting until later to deal with some of our sins.

Some try to hide or suppress what is happening on the inside and then call that holiness. We can play games with our thoughts or our actions, but the spirit of man is always true. What we are in our inner most being will bear fruit. No matter how much we try to suppress it, what is in our spirit will show up sooner or later in our thoughts or actions. It will show up in those around us. It will show up in our children. It will bear fruit. The tree of our inner man will produce apples, oranges, or whatever kind of tree it is. When the fruit shows up, we can identify the tree.

This is one of the most important principles in learning to follow the voice of the Spirit. We need to look for fruit instead of trying to monitor thoughts and actions. When we learn to be honest about what is showing up in our lives, we are setting a foundation for ownership that can then bring the connection that brings growth. Most people I know are going at it backwards. They try to change the actions, hoping that means that they have grown. God wants to connect in a way that will bring growth, which will then change the actions. When actions are the fruit of His presence, they are no longer just good flesh efforts, but truly carry the power of intimacy with Him that will bring glory to Him.

Spirit, Soul, and Body as Fruit

This does not mean that we focus entirely on our spirit and spiritual flow. We need to be attentive to all three levels: spirit, soul, and body. The soul and body need to be seen together with the spirit and not in isolation to get a more accurate view of what is actually happening. We can temporarily change our actions without ever completely dealing with our spiritual flow. A person can quit smoking by playing to a spiritual pride flow. He is better off physically for it, but remains unconnected because of the pride. In fact, in the spirit realm, he may be worse off overall. All thoughts and actions need to be seen in combination with spiritual flows. We need to renew the "spirit of the mind" and not just the thoughts themselves. We need to renew the spirit of the actions and not just the actions themselves. Everything happening at the soul and body level carries with it a spiritual anima-tion. The change process should include doing and thinking the right thing with the right spirit. We are heart human beings, and the heart cannot be divided three ways. Though I have focused in this book almost exclusively on spiritual flow, I have done so because it is largely missing from the Western Christian worldview. Thoughts and actions are just as much a part of the total heart makeup as spir-itual flow.

God is concerned with transforming the hearts of men. I advocate starting with a focus on connectedness to God, but that connectedness must develop into good thoughts, feelings, and actions. If a change in spiritual flow doesn't impact real life, it has been of no value.

The reason I give such strong emphasis to the flow of the spirit is because our culture has taught us that the starting point for spiritual change is words and actions. While good habits (like Bible reading!) are better than bad habits, the habit cannot be understood apart from the impact on the heart. I have run into many hardened persons in prison and in the church who were simply using Scripture to justify some selfish end. For them, even one of the best habits was being used to produce bad fruit.

God's Timetable

Because of the atonement, God is absolutely free to deal with each of us according to what will bring the greatest growth. He will leave some "sins" or points of immaturity till later. None of us is capable of instant maturity. The atonement removes the need for sin consciousness, and allows us to become God conscious. Our lives must be about getting and staying connected to the Spirit, and waiting for the time when that connection will bear good fruit.

Many get impatient waiting for the good fruit to come forth and try to turn to other means to force a positive response. They do not want to see themselves as still in bondage, nor do they want to be embarrassed in front of others. Rather than waiting on the fruit of God to manifest, they force the issue in some other way.

When we minister to someone who has had significant wounding, we will likely have a child on our hands. Arrested development is a fact. Though an adult, the person will act like a child and we will be disappointed that the process is not working. No! No! No! Getting a person connected will bear fruit. Not instantly; in some cases, not even quickly.

If an instantaneous victory brings pride and causes us to lose our connection, our victory becomes our defeat.

People we minister to may have to spiritually grow through the childhood years, then into the teen years, finally becoming an adult. The connection with God simply starts them on a growth pattern from whatever point that their development was shut down by their stronghold. The time it takes will usually be proportional to the depth of the bondage and the number of years in that bondage. God does accelerate the process even to the point of doing an instantaneous work at times.

It would be nice if we could see the instantaneous change in every situation, but I have found that God often makes us wait. He makes us obey Him one step at a time. He makes us connect one day—yes, even one minute—at a time. In many cases, I believe that growing in this discipline of needing to turn to Him is a part of the reason for the delay in seeing victory. We need to need Him. With instantaneous victories, sometimes we lose that perspective. With instantaneous victories, sometimes we become filled with pride and lose our ability to connect. When that happens, our victory becomes our defeat.

The important thing to remember is that the spirit of a man does not lie. His thoughts or actions may be a lie, but his spirit cannot lie. We can temporarily jump-start our outward holiness, but only connectedness with God produces fruit. When we learn to be in tune with our own spirit and with the spirits of others, we are preparing to be a true lifegiver. It will require great patience. It will require much waiting. Fruit takes time. We prefer an instant change in actions. We prefer outward holiness.

The child must be taught to obey his parents. There is a need for an outward response, but the godly parent knows what to require at what age. In spiritual circles we demand instant maturity of ourselves and of others. There is nothing more damaging to flowing in the spirit than this *demandingness* we place on ourselves and others.

We must learn to wait. It is God who gives us every good and perfect gift. When God asks us to obey, He enables us to obey. The flow of the Spirit will take us to the completion of the request. If we forsake the flow, we lose the ability to complete the request God's way and usually we try to complete it in some human way. We lose track of God and become brittle.

When we are ministering to others, a request for obedience to God should be accompanied by a spiritual flow of God's compassion through us to the person. If there is no enabling flow, we just may have to wait. It may not be time to tackle the problem just yet. After all, because of the atonement, the greatest problem is no longer sin. It is simply accepting what He has done for us and then returning to Him to do His bidding. We need to learn to stop weighting and start waiting for the One who will give us the signal that now is the time.

More Than We Can Deliver

I am not saying that outward behavior does not matter. God will continually be challenging a person to do what is just beyond his ability to complete. God's call cannot be completed without God's help. We tend to choose what we can complete and then become puffed up in spiritual pride. God chooses those things that are just beyond us so that we have to depend on Him.

The spiritual flow of a God-called task will hopefully be one of humility, thus producing both a good work and good spiritual fruit in our hearts. It is possible to get part of the way out there on a God mission and bail out of the spiritual flow. When that happens the person will either bail out on the obedience or will press through in human strength. Neither of those options establishes the life of God in the person.

Ultimately it takes the completion of the command to establish the good fruit that God desires. Right thoughts and right actions complete the work of God, but they are not the work of God. The work of God is an inclusive spirit, soul, and body work. The unified and whole person must be on board for a person to mature in Christ.

However, we do not necessarily get it right on our first attempt. On our first try, we may be doing well to just get connected for a time. On attempt number two the thoughts may come along. On attempt three the obedience may finally happen, but with the first success can come the spiritual pride that will then cause a fall shortly thereafter.

This is how it works. Each failure is an opportunity to reconnect, which is an opportunity to receive what is needed to grow toward maturity. When we get rid of the demandingness, and focus on staying connected in order to produce growth, it is a completely different lifestyle. Self-hatred and self-judgment are much less of an issue. As the demandingness begins to fade, we are more able to wait. And the ability to stay connected grows.

There are many in our culture who have never even stopped long enough to focus on the spiritual realm. They are completely consumed with the conscious realm of thoughts, feelings, and actions. Step one is to become more attentive to the spirit realm. Once we do that, the rest of what I am writing in this chapter will begin to make sense.

Being connected is not about being perfect or being without sin. It is not even an issue of being mature. It is about being a spiritual child or even a spiritual adult who has his eyes on God. God knows what we need at every stage.

This approach to life will not be "soft" in the area of holiness. God will stretch our level of holiness beyond what we would have ever thought possible. It will be a true holiness that originates in the heart, producing outward actions that are consistent with the commands of God. He is the author of the commands of the Bible. Do we truly think that if we live a life connected to Him that He will not lead us into holiness? The fruit of staying connected will be an ability to obey the commands, but obedience must be fruit and not a forced response.

Not Without Effort

There can be a middle stage where initial responses are a bit forced. I am not saying don't try to obey. We must add our efforts to the process. However, we must not be surprised by awkward attempts. We must eagerly anticipate the time when obedience is in full bloom. It takes all out human effort to obey along with the flow of the Spirit. The biggest difference in a dependent lifestyle is that the Spirit will continually challenge us to obey things that are slightly beyond us which will require His empowering to complete. We would tend to settle for things that are easily within our capabilities and then nurture spiritual pride.

To follow the voice of God requires flat out, full-blown effort. Sometimes that means that all of our energy must be focused on stilling our soul and waiting on God. Nothing should happen until we have a connection and a direction. Once we have our direction, it will require every bit of our physical, mental, and spiritual abilities to cooperate with God's request. In Christ, resting in the Spirit is not laziness. The Spirit connects, directs, and energizes. We respond with our whole being, but we do so in a way that can also be described as being connected to Him and in a state of resting in Him.

Following the voice of God is a full contact sport. It requires every ounce of our being. It is not a perfect science, but a pathway to maturity. At times, it can be advanced as much or more through failure than through seeming success. It is about learning to be saturated fully with the presence and substance of God. The more of Him we have, the better we hear since we do tend to hear according to our heart. The better we hear, the more we grow. It is a cycle that takes us from glory to glory. It is a spiritual sensing that allows us to participate in the growth of others.

Ministry is not about fixing people, but about growth in God. All true growth comes from being connected to God and moving with His will for our lives. When we are in His presence, manifesting His nature, we are in His will.

His will is much more about who we are and what we are than where we are. We tend to seek those questions: Where should I live? What job should I take? Who should I minister to? God says, "As you are going…minister to others" (a paraphrase of the Great Commission in Matt. 28:19–20). People get all up tight about being in the will of God as if it were a location. A far more important question is, "Are we connected?" And if so, "Are we using that connectedness to bless others?"

We do need to be directed as well as connected, but it is hard to lose His direction if we are truly connected. We want to be instantly mature, to be perfectly on track with God. Once we learn not to sweat the details so much, it is easier to relax and connect. In connecting is growth.

In case you hadn't figured it out, I am prone to press. I speak to myself with this book as much as I speak to others. God has had to teach me to wait. That is wait, not weight. I do the weight thing all too easily. I get heavy and I know that I am pushing God away. Ministry is not meant to be heavy, but light and life and joy.

One of the root words for the word *glory* means "to make weighty."[1] God does want us to be weighty, to be full of His substance, but not weighed down. In Him is glory, and life, and fullness of joy. His burden is easy. His load is light. In Him is the life of all men. Sometimes we just don't know how to appropriate that life. So tell me, are you weighting for God? Or truly waiting for God?

> *Lord, help me to recognize the difference between when it is me and when it is You working through me. God, I know that when I am the wrong kind of heavy, it is me. I rejoice that Your yoke is easy and Your burden is light. Fill me with Your energizing compassion. Amen. (Prayer based on Luke 9:55–56; Matthew 11:29–30.)*

Study Guide

1. How did pride hinder the author's ability to connect with God? What are some of the ways that pride impacted how he experienced life?

2. Give a description of the "sensing" of the voice of God. What makes this "sensing" accurate? What will make it inaccurate?

3. If you sense a disconnection with a person you are ministering to, or between the person and God, what should you do? When and how should you press on? When should you pull back?

4. How does waiting on God and others make us better prepared to minister? When we are willing to wait, what have we learned about ministry?

5. We all have tried to work holiness from the outside in. Is there an area in your life where you have struggled to obey? What is the spiritual flow that is animating this area? How could connectedness help you overcome in that area?

6. Are there areas where you have been impatient with yourself or others, where you just need to give time for maturity to take hold? How can you better apply this concept to your life? Where have you been too patient, not taking on the challenges of the Spirit to improve?

7. What is the role of human effort in the maturation process? How do we keep human effort from becoming a good flesh attempt to fulfill the commands of God?

Chapter 14

STEPS TOWARD LIFE

By now, you have probably figured out that I will not be promoting a traditional view of repentance, which seems to say to a person, "Just change." I believe that if it were that easy, more people would have already changed. The reality is that true change is not possible without some kind of help from the outside. We need God and we need people to help us through the process.

There are basically two theologies in play in the world of religion today. One theology tries to find a way to improve man to a god-like level. Buddhism does that. So does secular humanism. So do many of what mainstream Christians would classify as the cults. The second theology is very simply that God chooses to pour Himself into man. Man doesn't achieve god-likeness, he receives it as a gift, which in Christian terms we call grace. For Christians, the big question then is how do we "receive" His grace? If we are not careful, we create another "achieve" theology that mirrors those religions that we say we do not agree with.

Many teach repentance in that way. It is an elaborate work, a process of presenting yourself to God in a way that will make you acceptable. In Catholicism, there are a number of rituals thought necessary to present the believer worthy to enter the heavenly courts. In Protestant circles, we reduce the number of rituals down to just a few actions: what we call the prayer of salvation, followed by public confession, hopefully including baptism. The problem is that none of these outward rituals guarantee that any inward transformation has taken place.

"Receiving" Theology

If Christianity is truly about a "receiving" theology, we need to pay much more attention to the idea of connecting people to God, with ritual being nothing more than the outward completion of the inward transformation.

I will be describing seven different aspects of the transformation process. Though they are described as steps, they will not necessarily happen in order, but are different tools that we use at different times, or perhaps all at once. Their main purpose is to facilitate on-going connectedness to God. If these seven or any other set of actions become the pathway to God, do we truly have a "grace" theology? Are we really presenting anything different to the world than any other religion?

Too often, the answer is "No." We become more concerned with the ritual (or outward activity) rather than the reality of connectedness. "Have you prayed the sinner's prayer yet? OK, you're in!" What does a ritual prayer prayed in the past have to do with present reality? Becoming born again is about starting a relationship with God. If a person has prayed the sinner's prayer, but has no present reality of connectedness to God, something is wrong.

Yes, we need to get people saved and there is a starting point for salvation. But if the reality of the present relationship is stillborn, we need to help them just as much as if they were never born. It truly is about a present reality in a receiving theology. Are you in fellowship with God now? If not, something needs to change! Too many people in the church today have no such sense of a present reality of connectedness to Christ. Some never had it. They simply were told that they were saved after speaking a ritual prayer of salvation.

Each of the seven steps needs to be seen in light of this understanding. It is not about a ritual to be completed. The steps are tools to connect people to God. It may only take one tool on a given day. Or it may take all seven. Or none may be needed. Proper use of the tools will require the spiritual sensitivity of an intercessor, not the intellectual musings of a religious practitioner. Those connected to God should be able to sense God's leading to help them apply the right tool at the right time in the right way. It is the connection to

God that truly makes the difference, both for the intercessor and for the person in need.

1. Recognizing

If the steps are about connecting, where do we start? I believe one of the most basic steps in a receiving theology is seeing, or to keep the steps alliterative: recognizing. Those not born again cannot even see the kingdom of God. (See John 3:3.) As I described earlier, I believe that the way a person sees changes temporarily when that person receives of a godly presence and then begins the spiritual testing and tasting process.

Once this process has been activated, it is time for the intercessor to begin to work in the recognition area. It is important for the person we are working with to see himself clearly. It is important for the person to see God clearly. It is important for the person not just to see, but to download this new seeing, to own it, not just to play with it.

Midwifing God's Presence

In 1 John 1:8–9, it says, "If we say that we have no sin, we deceive ourselves, and the truth is not in us. If we confess our sins, He is faithful and just to forgive us our sins and to cleanse us from all unrighteousness." It is possible to take this verse and make a formula out if it, making step one in the ritual process as seeing the sin and step two as confession of sins. While that is accurate, I believe we need to think differently about the process. It is our job to midwife the presence of God connection that is beginning in the person. We don't create the process through intellectual connection; we bring it to a conscious level by coming along side what God is already doing.

A person who is newly experiencing a level of connectedness to God or to a godly person, will have a sense that things are not quite the way that he has been used to seeing them. He has been seeing life from an egocentric viewpoint. That is the way all of us work. Most of the time, our self-defense mode causes us to live in 1 John 1:8. We see ourselves as having no sin. We think of ourselves as being relatively OK, especially having good intentions even if we don't fully carry them out. Yes, I know. Some people have turned negative and are constantly attacking themselves instead. Yet, even this is a self-dependency, with the individual thinking that he is capable of self-monitoring. It is simply another way of excluding God or denying the need for God.

Connecting With the Ego's Reality

When godly presence is beginning to happen, and a recognition that the person may not be seeing life correctly begins to soak in, the intercessor is able to come along side the person and begin to explain a new reality. I have found, both in explanation and in prayer, one of the most effective ways to do this is to identify with the person's typical experience of reality. Seeing his typical spiritual flow, I begin to talk about the fear that he has been experiencing, or a sense of worthlessness, or a need to measure up. Again, these are presence kinds of approaches that should line up with his normal experience of life. If we, as intercessors, are truly seeing the individual and explaining what we are seeing, the person should be able to say a loud "Amen" once we have shared what we are seeing.

The typical approach to such a person is to try to intellectually convince him that he is in sin, and having convinced him of that fact, hopefully everything else changes. While this method does occasionally have success, I believe most of the time the success comes because of a "presence" connection. Intellectual discussions work if the person has entered into humility (a spiritual presence!). They don't work if the spirit is closed. Carefully observing spiritual flows is effective because our intellect tends to flow much more out of our presence than our presence does out of our intellect. They do affect each other, but the spiritual component is by far the stronger of the two.

A typical approach is to try to intellectually convince a person that he is in sin.

Describing to a person his typical experience of reality (like feeling very alone or feeling used) creates a great sense of connectedness with the person. There is a sense that "somebody finally understands me!" Or there is even a sense that "God really does see me!" Through this experience of spiritual connectedness, the person becomes even more open to an intercessor and to God who "really does see and understand what I have been going through." In this way, as intercessors, we actually begin to appeal to the ego instead of fighting against it. We come along side the person with understanding and connectedness instead of standing outside, demanding repentance.

Connecting With Biblical Reality

Once the level of connectedness has been strengthened, we can then begin to paint a picture of biblical reality, describing what God wants for the person in life. This can be done at least partially by learning to see from the negative flows to the positive potential. However, I am not describing a mechanical exercise so much as a Spirit led connection. If we are connected to God, He will guide us in creating vision for the person.

The person who has been feeling very isolated is not living in the will of God. He values relationship, and was created to be a relationship person, but has separated himself from everyone and is miserable. God's will for him is much better than where he has been. Unfortunately, we tend to take a "Que sera sera" view of God, thinking that whatever has happened must be the will of God for the person.

An intercessor begins to create vision of how God really wants it to be for the person. He explains to the person in need that what currently is happening in the person's life is not the will of God. The will of God is love, joy, and peace in the Holy Spirit. When this concept begins to soak in, it definitely represents a change in seeing.

The person will now be able to start recognizing the will of God and the hand of God. He will also begin to recognize the role of self that is blocking the very presence of God.

It is helpful, at this stage, to explain to the person the concept of spiritual presence, that we are created to house a spiritual presence, and that we can only house one presence at a time. Unforgiveness and forgiveness cannot coexist. We may move back and forth, but we can only consistently house one presence at a time. If the person then begins to "Amen" that his spiritual presence is one of feeling "all alone" (or any other presence not compatible with God's presence), he will begin to see how this has excluded God from the picture. Ownership is beginning to happen. The person begins to see that he has chosen an egoistic presence that in turn has excluded God's presence.

This is a huge step toward the recognition needed if progress is going to be made. It is essential for the person to see his role in blocking out God's presence in order for him to have any hope for change. Seeing that he has excluded God helps him to change his view of God to that of a more interested and loving Father. Seeing that it is his choices of spiritual flow that have blocked out God's help brings ownership for the life that he has lived. Most people blame others or God for the way their life has gone.

It is essential for the person to see his role in blocking out God's presence.

The goal of this recognition area is not just to get the person to see himself as a miserable sinner so much as it is to prepare him to receive from God. He needs to see himself as a person with potential in God. He needs to see that his potential is only activated and completed by experiencing the on-going presence and strengthening of God. And he needs to see God as ready and willing to offer help to him, if he will only humble himself and ask for help. Done right, the person truly sees himself as having fallen short of the image and glory of God. (See Romans 3:23.) He also sees his potential of being restored to that glory over time as he embraces the Spirit's work. We typically have done a good job of getting people to see what they are doing wrong, but not nearly as good a job getting them to see what they could be in Christ.

2. Repenting

Having laid this groundwork, the repentance area should not be overly difficult, but again, we need to focus on the spiritual, not just specific actions. I believe most traditional sin areas actually are an outgrowth of a wrong spiritual flow. Too often, we have people repenting for drug use, when the deeper need is to address unforgiveness, spiritual pride, or self-pity. They do need to repent for both the inward and the outward, but the inward is the more critical of the two.

While it is true that at times failure in the major sin areas will bring a person to our doorsteps for ministry, if we focus only on the outward response, I believe we miss a great opportunity to put the person on a track for growth. It is connectedness to God that will bring growth. In some instances, the drug use may be the major cause for the disconnection, but in most cases there are far deeper spiritual substance and spiritual presence issues that need to be addressed. If we only focus our attention on a single outward sin and ask for repentance from that sin, we miss a chance to be more thorough, a chance to get the person reconnected to God in a way that will truly help.

To build vision in a person who needs to repent, we need to remember that our greatest weaknesses usually grow out of our greatest strengths. A person's area of bondage is a perversion of his gifting and calling. The servant overcommits in service, becomes bitter, and closes himself off from the very people God has called him to serve.

A Vision for Serving God

True repentance is not just about feeling sorry for a sin, but is an embracing of the call of God, and also an acknowledgement of God's right to be Lord over every single part of our lives. Repentance that creates a positive vision for serving God is much more powerful than a repentance coming out of feeling like a no one and a nobody. Vision and value are two of our greatest tools. They can be used in every single thing that we do.

For those who would say that harsh and negative confrontation works, I do have to concede that there are times when being harsh appears to be the key to transformation. If a person is a rebel, a harsh response fits the way that God responds to the person in order to possibly trigger humility. If humility is triggered, the person is now in a position to receive, and the visioning and valuing process must then take over for life to be passed to the other person.

A person who has never been connected to God, or who has struggled with a great degree of bondage, will struggle believing God could move in him and through him. It is not faith in God that hinders most of us. James tells us that even the demons believe in God. (See James 2:19.) The greater issue is almost always an inability to believe that God will actually come and do a work in our lives. Our past experience often tells us that God won't be there for us. He has not been there in the past. Why should He show up now? Getting a person to see a more accurate picture of the loving Father is needed for true repentance, which is turning to God in faith, and abandoning of self into the hands of a loving God.

The biggest battle is not usually seeing that there is sin, though in this society many people are in a state of denial about the concept of sin. The bigger battle generally is getting the person to believe that he can be different. Most people choose not to believe they are in sin, because they see no potential for help on the other side. I believe that most who deny sin actually do so for egoistic reasons. They are protecting themselves from a sense of failure. Repentance acknowledges the failure, but it also should bring a hope for change. The hope for change may need to precede the acknowledgement of sin or failure. I know that sounds backwards, but I have found that it works. Romans 2:4 tells us that it is the goodness of God that leads us to repentance.

Repentance is a person setting his face toward doing the will of God. It is not the completion of the task. It is the setting of a direction, the embracing of God's vision. The empowerment to complete the task will come later. This is a hard step for the person, because the ego does not want to commit to anything that might represent a future failure. Not only that, God will be asking for the person to do what has been impossible for him to do in the past. Can you see that repentance done right is a huge step of faith for a person? Instead, we often settle for remorse, and a few human baby steps—that the person thinks he can accomplish on his own.

The hope for change may need to precede the acknowledgment of sin or failure.

Repentance done right brings the person to a point of dealing with anything that is currently blocking the flow of the presence of God. We must learn not to stop with a person feeling sorry for some way in which he really blew it. Most want to focus on a single bad behavior, go through a ritual of great anguish, and then think they are done with repentance. We must look for deeper substance issues that block service to God and man. And it is not as if every single thing has to be cleaned up in one session. God has an order. Even as a child acquires skills in a sequential order, so will the new believer. We need to find His order and direct the person to those issues that are currently on His agenda. Some things will have to wait for a later time, but if the presence of God is restored we can generally have confidence that we have reached our goal in the repentance area.

3. Releasing

Once a person has pointed his face toward the will of God for his life, there often is a huge obstacle called unforgiveness. In several of the parables, God has made it very clear that if we do not forgive men, God will not forgive us. Connecting is the key to transformation. Any kind of holding on to the past will prevent us from moving forward into God's future.

Our world has so perverted the idea of forgiveness that we now think that if we forgive something, we are saying, "It's OK." If someone has sinned against you, it is not "OK." Sin is sin. It is grotesque. What God wants us to do is to let Him be the master and the judge. We must let go of the situation. We must release it to Him.

Release is an incredible word to describe what needs to happen. I believe it better describes forgiveness in our culture than the word forgiveness. We let go. The next stage will be receiving from God. That cannot happen unless we let go.

Release is more than just letting go of hurts. It is letting go of faith in self. It is letting go of faith in human institutions. It is utterly abandoning our future to a loving God who will take care of us. This is a simple step, but a powerful one.

Too many people try to walk in faith without having fully come to a point of surrender to God. Faith without having first surrendered is nothing more than the person playing God. Many walk around saying, "I am healed," without having gone through the surrender process. They read the Word and assume a future without fully giving that future to God. While I believe it is God's will to heal, being adamant about something that you read in the Word is not the same thing as faith. Being adamant is playing God. Surrendering and coming to a point of being able to rest in God is a much better pathway to faith. True release is vital and almost always comes before the gift of faith into our hearts!

4. Receiving

This brings us to what I believe is the pivotal step: receiving. So far, everything has been focused toward this time and it needs to be! If a person doesn't sense a connectedness to God, all we are doing is giving him a Christian philosophy and telling him to go and live better than he used to live. There is no power in Christian philosophy. It merely stirs up human effort, which if successful will lead to spiritual pride.

Becoming Children

God's solution is a real contact with Him. Those saved should have the experience of Romans 8:15–16, "For you did not receive the spirit of bondage again to fear, but you received the Spirit of adoption by whom we cry out, 'Abba, Father.' The Spirit Himself bears witness with our spirit that we are children of God." The gospel of grace is the good news of empowerment.

What a person could not do before he repented, he should be able to do after repentance because of the empowering work of the Holy Spirit. Before repentance, verse 15 talks about fear dominating the person's life. After connection to God a sense of belonging to God dominates. Where fear or hatred once dominated a person, there is now a new energy to be bold or to love because of the quickening of the Holy Spirit. The one who was lost spiritually knows that he is no longer lost because of the witness of the Spirit. The one who had been trapped in sin now feels the presence and the power of the gospel. This is truly the hope of the gospel. It is real in experience and not just in print.

New Ability

If there is no ability to move forward in righteousness, either there are some other unrecognized strongholds or the person lacks the connection with God that will truly empower him to change. There is a third reason why the person might not move forward. He does have to want to move forward. A lack of desire will block the connection with God. God has to be invited before He will enter. I hesitate to even mention the "want to" because when a breakthrough is not happening, we are often quick to try to push blame off on the one we are ministering to. We need to bypass the blame game and ask God for wisdom when there is a blockage.

Some who start the process of moving toward God do so primarily because they have felt a connection and empathy from the intercessor. Once into the process, they are not sure they are ready for a full surrender to God. Sometimes that means we wait. Sometimes the person bails out completely. If the person stops short of true connectedness, he will lack the ability he needs to overcome areas of bondage. If the person does connect, the power needed to overcome will be present.

So many today are afraid of promising empowerment through receiving to a person. It puts the reality of Christianity on the line. Instead, they choose to treat Christianity as a mere philosophy and hope that the good advice of the Bible will get the job done. A person trapped in sin is trapped. That is what the Scriptures tell us. (See Romans 6:16.) He is in bondage. That bondage is not going to just go away with a better effort. We must introduce the power of God into the situation.

Many are afraid to promise this because they are not walking in presence and power themselves. Some are not willing to extend the promise of His strengthening because they have never learned to sense and flow in the realm of spiritual presence. They were taught to approach Christianity as a mere philosophy and know little of the empowering of Christ. Some have blockages of their own and thus have not learned to connect, nor are even aware that connecting is possible. We must become people of faith and get beyond these obstacles. We are to carry the power of the gospel to people, not empty words. (See 1 Corinthians 2:4–5.)

Many that we minister to will need some major explanation of the spiritual realm before they can connect spiritually. I often use words like peace and joy to describe a sensing of the spiritual flow and then I distinguish the spiritual from the soulish—joy from mere happiness. It is helpful if the person is attentive toward the right thing. If we talk about being touched by God, or hearing God's voice, many are expecting a thought to go neon inside of them. Instead, the voice of God is usually a presence that "bears witness" (Rom. 8:16) on the inside of the person, leaving him with a sense of peace and connectedness. Out of that inner peace comes the power to live a new life.

Receiving Is Non-Negotiable

This receiving stage has to become a non-negotiable. If for some reason, we cannot help midwife the connection with a first time of ministry, we must not give up. Through prayer and fasting, we should be able to see a breakthrough in the lives of those who are genuinely seeking. There have been very few times that I have had to go past the first time of ministry to see God connect with His people. He wants to connect with us far more than we want to connect with Him. Repentance and faith are needed. Open arms are needed. He will do the rest, especially if we begin to expect that to be the normal outcome.

Being spiritual is being connected.

By now, the main point of the book should be obvious: to be spiritual is to connect. Everything we do, and even the way we do things should lead to restoration of relationship with God and man. These first four steps generally will have brought about the initial connection to God. The final three steps help the person move from temporary presence to permanent download. However, I want to reiterate that we are not just talking about mechanical steps, but steps toward life, steps toward reconnecting, steps toward God. It is the same old stuff of recognition, repentance, release, and receiving, but a spiritual worldview changes everything. Relationship is life. Are you taking steps toward life?

> *Father God, I realize that it is Your heart for me to reflect Your glory. I also realize that I have fallen short of Your glory and that the only way for me to return to that place is to connect with You. I need You continually. You are my glory. Amen. (Prayer based on Romans 3:23.)*

Study Guide

1. What are the two primary theologies active in the world today? How is Christianity a completely unique theology from all other religions?

2. Instead of being as concerned with whether or not a person has prayed the sinners prayer, what does this chapter say we should be concerned about? Do you agree or disagree and why do you feel that way?

3. What does this chapter say is likely to trigger the recognition process? If that is true, what do we need to do to challenge people to see differently?

4. What is equally as important for the potential believer as seeing his sin area? How can we foster this seeing in a person?

5. When dealing with repentance, how do we get beyond specific sins and begin to identify spiritual substance and spiritual presence issues? What approach can we take that will not likely be offensive to the other person?

6. For many, a major obstacle is simply beginning to recognize the spiritual realm within them and learning to connect with God's Spirit in them. In your own words, how would you communicate to another person how to recognize the moving of God's Spirit in his life?

7. Describe a few seasons in your life when God has moved upon you in each of the four steps.

Chapter 15

CLOSING ACCESS POINTS

D avid was angry. In fact, David's anger could be more accurately described as rage. The fool Nabal had just humiliated his servants. He and his men had been good to Nabal. They could have raided his flocks for their own food, but instead they had protected them. Now at the time of sheep shearing, he had merely asked to take part in what was considered to be normal hospitality. Instead, Nabal had turned away David's men with rough and humiliating words.

In his rage, David had made a vow to execute all the males of Nabal's household before morning light and was riding furiously toward the execution of his vow. Abigail, Nabal's wife, threw herself down before David and pleaded for mercy. Part of her argument was simple: "David, do you really want this blood on your hands? When you become king, will the people gladly follow someone who killed a kinsman from the tribe of Judah over such a trivial thing?"

In 1 Samuel 25:33, David responds, "And blessed is your advice and blessed are you, because you have kept me this day from coming to bloodshed and from avenging myself with my own hand." Those last few words are very significant. David was called a man after God's own heart because he lived most of his life with a constant awareness that God was right there looking over his shoulder. He also realized that, if possible, God did so in order to bless him. If he carried on with this plan, it would be of his "own hand" and could not be blessed by God.

The next step in the seven R's is not so much a regular part of the process as it is a tool to be used at critical times in our lives. It is needed to remove blockages and to release the next growth burst of the believer. For David, the next growth burst was to start thinking like a king. He could no longer respond as a raider running from a king and be blessed. The days were growing short until he would take over as king, and David needed to grow.

Breaking Satan's Hold

The very second that we come to Jesus, Satan's ability to attack us is significantly hampered. However, the reality is that any area of our lives that is not completely dedicated to God is still a point of access for Satan. If we have not fully surrendered a spouse or a child to God, Satan can play on our fears. Fear is a spiritual flow that allows Satan access to our spirit, even though we are covered by the blood of Jesus. David had taken an offense toward Nabal on behalf of his men. That too was an access point for Satan. Because of these access points, we can be headed for heaven and be completely clean in the eyes of the Father (see John 15:3), and still be open to Satanic attack.

Every person who is on the verge of breaking through to a life-style of walking in the goodness of God has to stand up to the attacks of the enemy. Satan is a defeated foe, but we are the ones who will have to take the steps necessary to enforce the victory that Jesus has already won. As we start to understand the lifegiver model, we understand that there are many things lurking in our hearts that potentially give Satan access to us. It would be nice if we could take a stand once and for all and totally vanquish the enemy, but that is not how it works. On a daily basis, life will probe areas that may not have been fully given to God. Anything that is not fully consecrated to Him is a potential access point.

We don't even recognize most of these access points until they are in our face because of a life experience. In fact, that is why I believe God allows us to be tested. Not so that we will fail, but so that we can see the legal grounds that Satan could potentially use to destroy us in some future event. If we see it, we can then take back that ground.

David needed to see his impulsive nature and rein it in. Perhaps if he had seen his impulsive nature on a broader scale, he would have been prepared to handle the Bathsheba incident in a better way. But that is another story. Renouncing is about laying the legal foundation necessary to defeat the attacks of the enemy.

5. Renouncing

If a person has dedicated himself to something other than God, he needs to renounce that dedication. The greater the involvement the person has had with the demonic or in making unholy vows, the more necessary the act of renouncing becomes. It is a spiritual authority issue. David vowed an unholy vow, and would have carried it out had it not been for Abigail. We, too, need to look for the Abigail's in life who are pointing out areas of dedication to unholy tasks. Like David, we need to stop short, renounce those things, and rededicate ourselves to the glory of God. Every one of us was created to serve the One who created us. Anything less than total dedication to God is a breaking of the first commandment. We must return to our created purpose of serving and worshiping our God.

Dedication

The actual step of renouncing is easy. The first part is a repentance for not serving God and then a dedication of self back to God: "God, I was created to serve You. Instead, I have connected with, chose, or served _____. God, forgive me. I humble myself now and dedicate myself to You." The second part is the renouncing of the unholy vow or demonic involvement. An unholy vow is a statement like, "I will never allow myself to be hurt again." God clearly says that we must suffer with Him in order to serve Him. This kind of vow cannot be scriptural. To resolve this kind of vow, there needs to be a statement of a willingness to suffer with Christ if need be, and a statement like, "God, I trust You to walk me through every difficult situation." Most unholy vows come in some form of "I will never..."

It is also helpful for the renouncing to include an absolute dedication of the future to God, and a cutting off of any further involvement with the demonic. Any deliberate involvement with the demonic, whether through games, music, or direct involvement in the occult is an open door for the demonic to torment a person. Until these things are renounced, they act as a spiritual access point. It is as if Satan can cause a person's radio dial to jump to his station of spiritual darkness through the access point of the open door.

This is hard for people to understand, but the analogy with our substance being written on an internal hard drive is helpful. Past involvements with the occult don't just disappear at salvation. Salvation comes through a connection with God. There is a current presence. There is a new God download on the hard drive, but it is not a download to end all downloads. Our old substance is there on our hard drives. New substance must overwrite the old over time. Each time an item is replaced, permission must be given.

Any involvement that we have had with the occult or with unholy vows is like a file written on the hard drive. When the right trigger comes along, Satan is able to bring that file up into our current presence and use it to try to regain his authority over us. The file is an access point. It is an open door to Satan. That file needs to be closed. Destroyed. Overwritten. Gone.

Cutting off the Legal Ground

That is what renouncing is all about. It is the willful closing of the access points that Satan has held in the past. Because the individual is the one who surrendered his authority to Satan, only the individual has the ability to break the access point. Thus, renouncing requires speaking directly to the demonic, not to God. An example is something like this: "Satan, I have repented and dedicated myself to God in this area. I renounce any future involvement in this area. I have no right to involve myself with you in any way. I am a child of God and I am fully dedicated to Him. I cut you off from my life. You have no authority over me. I command you to leave me. I have repented of my sin in this area, and I am washed clean by the blood of Jesus. I am free in Him and I command you to leave." (It is helpful to specifically name the sin or occult involvement in this prayer instead of the general language that I have given.)

Exerting Our Authority

Many do not like to take this step in the manner that I am describing. They prefer to pray some sort of prayer toward God, asking Him to do something about the situation. However, it is the person who entered into the wrong participation with the demonic. Only that same person can undo that connection. Repentance toward God and a pleading with Him to do something about it is not adequate.

Satan will recognize the weakness of the individual who is pleading with God, and will turn up his tactics of intimidation. At this point in the process, it is the person who is the seat of authority and not God. A silent prayer does not exercise authority in the spiritual realm. God hears our silent prayers, but renouncing is about taking authority over the devil. The devil only responds to spiritual authority.

When we cut off any past activity with the demonic or with unholy vows and dedicate ourselves to God, we cut off the devil's authority to attack us. But as I said before, Satan still loves to intimidate. Only if we begin to enforce that authority change will Satan back off. We must speak it, not just think it. And we might need to speak it a second or a third time, or even continually for a time in order to build our own faith in our ability to exercise the authority God has given us as believers. Once we confess our sins and dedicate ourselves to God, we are clean. Satan has no authority over us. We must believe that and stand on it!

Even so, the person's will must be clearly expressed to the spiritual realm. The first time we speak that will to the spiritual realm, it is authoritative, but we speak it additional times to build our faith and to back off the intimidation of the devil. When we are new in the Lord, God will tend to protect us from that intimidation for a season, but as we grow, He wants us to learn to exercise our authority.

However, it is important to remember that there are things that God cannot do for a person. He cannot repent on behalf of a person.

He cannot make the dedication pronouncement. Nor can He enforce the permanent victory over Satan for us. He can and will insulate us from attack for a season if we need it. He does see our heart, even in unspoken prayers. He comes when invited. He strengthens. He helps but He cannot do the renouncing step for us. There are times when God has placed things in our hands. In those times, we are the ones who must speak to see a change.

I have found this to be a hard concept for many believers to grasp. They want God to take care of the problem, or they want to pray silently. Usually I have believers who are new at this sort of thing repeat a prayer after me. If they are spiritually connecting with the prayer, it is authoritative. But they have to speak it. The intercessor cannot speak it for them or over them. It is the spoken word of the cleansed saint that seals the "Amen" and secures the victory. The intercessor can help nurture the deliverance from evil, but he cannot actually do it himself.

The hard part about this step is identifying all the areas that need to be renounced.

The hard part about this step is identifying all the areas that need to be renounced. As I said earlier, some will need little or no work in the renouncing area. In general, I tend to look at this stage mostly when there is unexplainable blockage in what should be a normal flow of the presence of God. If there is no flow, we start looking for the cause, which may be in this area of demonic oppression. Also, if information gathered during ministry points to involvements that have given authority to Satan, renouncing is a good idea before the blockage hits.

In today's world, demonic involvement can be difficult to track. There was a time when it could be identified mostly through "harmless" games or activities that had some sort of direct occult tie, such as horoscopes, Ouija boards, or tarot cards. Today, some of the greatest entrance points are in the areas of drugs and pornography. Dealers of this filth have learned that incantations of the demonic pronounced over their products multiply the level of bondage and help guarantee future customers. Because of the dark side of these products, intertwining the demonic is quite simple. I generally assume the need for renouncing if any of these kinds of things have ever been used in a person's life.

Some Other Access Points

However, there are some entry points for the demonic that are much more subtle. When a person's spirit is at a point of complete openness and he is lacking the protection of the Spirit of God, he is potentially vulnerable to a demonic connection that will oppress him. One entry point that we would not think of is a trauma. Fear is negative faith. Faith is God's normal access point to our spirits, but in a similar way, faith in the negative can be an open door to the demonic. A severe trauma can be a point for the demonic to attach itself to a person. Whenever that traumatic spiritual climate is triggered, the demonic is able to overtake the person and produce actions through the person that are seemingly out of the person's control. When Satan has clear access points to us, we can temporarily or even permanently lose control to him. To obtain victory is simply a matter of finding those access points, dedicating them to God, renouncing any future involvement with the darkness, and commanding Satan to leave.

Another subtle access point for the darkness is through the generations. A close relative's involvement in the demonic often becomes an access point for Satan for the descendents. Just as the parent is given a great ability to influence the spiritual future of his child, even so one involved in the occult can pass that influence to a close relative. Again, there has to be some kind of "Amen" by the relative, but in the case of the demonic that too can be very subtle. Satan doesn't wait for us to hand over the keys willingly. If he can take us by force, he will. Sometimes this can happen through a single traumatic experience.

Anyone who is passive becomes a candidate for Satan's oppression, especially if there is an open door from the generations. I mostly look for generational situations when all other explanations have been exhausted. If I have tried the normal avenues and there seems to be no success, I start asking questions about relatives. Another clue to the probability of a generational open door is heightened spiritual sensitivity. The person who is hypersensitive spiritually likely inherited that sensitivity, either from someone walking very close to God, or someone who had opened the door to the demonic.

Another open door for the demonic is through some of the forms of meditation being practiced today. The goal of especially the Eastern meditation forms is to reach a point of inactivity and passivity. Passivity is always an invitation to the demonic. Satan is no gentleman, and he will take by force what a person would never give him. The Christian parallel to passivity is an active surrender. For the Christian, meditation should be focused toward God with an active sense of, "I am here to serve You, O God." The one who is spiritually looking to God and inviting His presence will have His protection.

Meditation that moves a person toward complete passivity is dangerous.

Meditation is not dangerous. It is biblical. Meditation that moves a person toward complete passivity is dangerous. Passivity leaves the door to the spirit wide open. The passive person is in danger of being manipulated by Satan even outside of meditation, though the access to the spirit is more open with intentional passivity than with the more unintentional variety.

Dedication to God

In each of these areas, the key is a closing of the door to the demonic and a replacing of that open door with a dedication to God. The name of Jesus and the blood of Jesus are effective and powerful tools. Used with faith, they will break the hold of the demonic and help create a new flow of the Spirit, a new sense of connectedness to God. If there has been demonic oppression, the person will definitely testify to having a new sense of freedom when that oppression is broken. "Therefore if the Son makes you free, you shall be free indeed" (John 8:36).

For those who have willfully contacted the demonic and dedicated themselves to the power of darkness, the process is similar but there is likely to be a much greater level of intercession and spiritual warfare needed to bring freedom to the person. In cases of willful surrender to darkness, Satan's authority level is much greater. The number of surrender points in the person's life is likely to be more numerous, and there are likely multiple trigger points. Because of this, it takes a much more thorough and powerful approach to bring freedom. We must enter these confrontations with caution, having prayed, fasted, and definitely having the leading of God to move ahead.

Protection Through Exposure

Life is our teacher. Like David, we will find ourselves headed off on a mission, only to be called up short. The fool continues on his mission even after its motives have been exposed as not being of God. The fool lives by his "own hand." The wise man completely dedicates himself to God and waits for the blessing of God in His time.

David's needs were met through Abigail. Nabal died a rather mysterious death ten days later, which once again pointed out to David the futility it would have been to take matters into his own hand. When we see God's hand in all things, we understand that God is exposing those access points that Satan wants to use to destroy us.

We typically see nothing but the offense. God sees the potential for protection and blessing and removes His hand so that the access point can be exposed and then removed. Anything not fully dedicated to God is a danger point. David's impulsive nature was one of those danger points. God exposed it and David humbled himself. If God is removing His hand of protection, there is a reason. We have an open door that is giving authority to the enemy. Most of the time I talk about the value of keeping your spirit open, but this is one time where it is a good thing to have the doors shut and locked!

God, help me to understand that a surrendered life is the safest life of all. In all things, I desire to humble myself before You and to give You all my cares, that in due time, You will lift me up to the place of Your glory. Amen. (Prayer based on 1 Peter 5:6–7.)

Study Guide

1. What is the primary purpose of renouncing? When is renouncing needed? What does renouncing do for the believer?

2. What are three basic parts of the renouncing process? How do these parts all tie in with the first commandment?

3. What is an "unholy vow"? What form do they usually take? What causes them to form and how are they reversed?

4. Why does renouncing need to include the part of directly speaking to the demonic realm? How does speaking it out loud make a difference?

5. This chapter says, "Life is our teacher." How does life show us when renouncing might be needed?

6. If a person wanted to do a thorough cleansing of areas that might give Satan authority, what are some of the typical areas that might give Satan authority?

7. Many people struggle with speaking out loud as a part of this activity. Are there areas of your life where Satan is harassing you and you still need to make a clear, verbal pronouncement of your current and future dedication to God, and then completely cut off Satan's authority? What do you need to get to a point of victory in this area?

Chapter 16

MIDWIFING THE LIFE

Getting a person to a point of tasting the presence of God is one thing; establishing that presence as a solid, ongoing godly substance in the person is another. Hezekiah is a great example of a man who had come out of a messed up background to make something of himself and of his nation. His father, Ahaz, had set up idols in the temple and eventually had closed down the temple altogether. The young King Hezekiah turned all of that around and turned a nation back to God.

Then came the test. Sennacherib of Assyria was closing in on Jerusalem. Israel had already been carried off into captivity. A panicked Hezekiah sent messengers to Isaiah speaking the following words: "Thus says Hezekiah: 'This day is a day of trouble, and rebuke, and blasphemy; for the children have come to birth, but there is no strength to bring them forth'" (2 Kings 19:3).

One of the greatest struggles in helping a person to a point of repentance is getting that person to believe that God will help bring positive change in his life. Most of us know God can. We just don't believe that He will. We prefer to live in our good flesh efforts over risking faith in God's intervention. And why should we give repentance another try when we have failed so many times before, especially if we have no reason to believe God will suddenly intervene this time? Satan takes advantage of this human tendency and jumps all over our moment of weakness to try to keep us in bondage. Once a person sees and cooperates with the spiritual realm, there is hope. There are good results. There is a connection to God. It is different.

After a person has repented and begun to serve God, the next tactic of the devil is frequently intimidation. The authority of the demonic has been cut off, but not the intimidation. When Sennacherib was closing in, Satan prompts Hezekiah to ask questions like, "Has it been worth it to serve God? Will He let me down in my hour of need?" Or a little more directly from the Scriptures, "Have we brought this thing to the point of birth only to see the baby die?"

Breaking Through Fears

I believe that this is the fear of every man who is on the verge of breaking through to a lifestyle of walking in the goodness of God. We see the sacrifices that we have made, and we start to ask questions. Satan senses a point of weakness, and he goes after it with all he has. He knows this is the critical point in the battle. He has been legally defeated by the repentance. He has been practically defeated by the receiving stage, but as long as the illusion of his control remains, he can intimidate a person back into the old areas of bondage. The baby is at the point of birth, but will it come through the delivery alive?

This gives us an excellent perspective on the final two steps of ruling and resting. These two steps are needed to enforce the victory, to maintain the connection, and to defeat the cruel intimidation of the enemy of our souls. The victory was won at the cross and is being appropriated through the recognizing, releasing, repenting, and receiving stages. But it must be established through the words and the life of the individual, who now has the authority to become a child of God. (See John 1:12.) The authority has been given, but it is our "Amen" that will complete the download, that will remove the enemy's remaining hold over us. Renouncing was the first step in this process. Ruling and resting are the final two steps.

6. Ruling

Ruling is about enforcing the victory we have already received in Christ. This step also is more up to the person and more of an "after care" activity because it has to continue happening in the person's on-going life choices. He has to stay in the place of victory, which only happens with an active engaging of God and an active denial of the demonic.

We must prepare the person for success in the ruling area. God's purpose in this whole process is to change a heart, to complete a download of His image onto our hard drive, to transform our character so that there are no open doors to the demonic. The first four steps will help a person achieve godly spiritual presence. Achieving a level of presence brings minimal change. Continually walking in that presence brings lasting change. This may be the most important step, but because most of it happens outside of the direct contact with the intercessor, it is often forgotten.

Proverbs 16:32 says, "He who is slow to anger is better than the mighty, and he who rules his spirit than he who takes a city." The upright man is spiritually in touch with God and under submission to God. He is also able to extend the authority of God to rule and reign over the fleshly urges that would rise up and try to take over his spiritual presence and his thinking, feelings, or actions. Godliness begins with ruling and reigning over its own individual space, that is our own bodies. We then extend that authority in a proper way to those around us. The person who has been oppressed by some level of darkness is usually doing well just to break through to the presence of God, let alone being expected to walk continually in that godly presence as a truly upright person would.

Ruling Is Maturing

It is not realistic to expect a person to move from a pattern of darkness (like worry!) to a pattern of light (like faith) without the appropriate spiritual weightlifting. They have to be helped to a point of strength. They have to be gradually moved toward a point of maturity, which is the place of being able to rule and reign over those urges. The recognition, repentance, releasing, receiving, and renouncing steps are almost automatic and instantaneous to the one who has reached maturity in an area.

Those who are mature know how to resist the devil, thus staying in constant fellowship with God and receiving from Him the empowerment to live a victorious life. Victory is not about a person becoming stronger in himself. When self is the source of strength, no one is able to fight off the sin nature and the demonic realm. There is some ability for a person to grow and to rule and reign by accessing the "good treasure" of the heart, but that ability is limited. Apart from God, we all are subject to the law of sin and death. (See Romans 8:2.) We are all subject to a continual descent into sin. Only in Christ do we have the power to overcome the law of sin and death.

Learning to rule works according to the pattern of Romans 8:13: "For if you live according to the flesh you will die; but if by the Spirit you put to death the deeds of the body, you will live." In the first part of the verse, it plainly states that if we give our flesh part the authority to rule, that it will bring death—spiritual death. That is separation from God. Again, notice how weakness and passivity bring death. The one who gives in to the flesh dies. When Satan's tool of intimidation does not work, he can only hope that we wimp out in our fight against sin. If we don't take authority over it, it will take authority over us—saved or not saved.

Our hope for victory begins with the phrase, "if by the Spirit." We are not left to ourselves. When we recognize our sin and through repentance turn our eyes back to God, we set ourselves up to receive from the Spirit of God. We are directly connected to God Himself. We are no longer a battery depending on our own power, but we are connected to a power station full of glory and life. Recognition, repentance, release, and receiving activate the "if by the Spirit." Renouncing removes any remaining hindrances. We are connected and ready.

You Rule by the Spirit

Now comes the part of that verse that is easy to miss: "you." "If, by the Spirit...*you*." It is not God who will rule and reign. He has assigned that role to us. God will not come in and kill the flesh for us. That is our job. He cannot and will not do it. We are the ones who must say the "Amen!" to God by recognizing our sin and turning to Him. We are the ones who must get a grip on those fleshly urges that would try to overtake us. We are the ones who must speak out loud to the demonic when it is trying to intimidate us. We must take the authority.

God can't and won't do it for us because His purpose is to transform our hearts. That transformation does not take place without our direct participation. He provides the Spirit. He strengthens. We must say the "Amen." *We must believe He has appropriated the power to us.* We must rule! But we cannot rule until the contact with the Spirit is a reality and the needed cleansing has been done.

It is one thing to tell a person to get a grip on life, to tell him to "just grow up!" It is another thing to help him get there. We are not to demand a performance so much as to midwife the growth toward being able to rule over the flesh. A primary key to victory in the ruling stage is vision. If the fleshly urges have our attention, we will begin to build visions that line up with those urges. The worrier will begin to imagine all kinds of terrible possibilities. The one controlled by lust will indulge in some rather unseemly fantasies.

Vision and Focus

Our vision tends to lead us to a destination. Focus leads to a destination. The power to focus is, I think, the greatest weapon in the arsenal of the mature person, the one who has the ability to rule and reign. "What you see is truly what you will get," and what you see will be determined by which direction you are looking. Those who have truly repented and have their eyes on God will see one vision. Those who have allowed the flesh to creep back in will be seeing visions that line up with the flesh.

We "put to death" the flesh by getting connected to God, and then destroying anything that would try to rise up to cut us off from that presence. The worrier will almost instantly want to fall back into old thought patterns. Because our minds tend to work in habitual patterns, the old thought life is a part of the flesh that will have to be put to death by the person. How? Our thought life is best renewed by the Word of God. For the worrier, a good verse would be "Be anxious for nothing, but in everything by prayer and supplication, with thanksgiving, let your requests be made known to God" (Phil 4:6). The key once again is focus. If the worrier changes his focus from his worries to a verse like this, and disciplines himself to focus on the Word, a new thought pattern begins to emerge. A new vision emerges. A new set of emotions emerge. A new set of actions begin to take shape.

I believe the Word of God is an absolute key to this area of ruling and reigning. If the stronghold area has been identified, the person needs to find a good (or several!) antidote verse and memorize it. It can be posted around the house, in the car, at the office, etc. The vision and concepts behind the Word must become the new focus. The Word needs to create a new anticipation of the future and how it is to be lived and how it *will* be lived. What we see will determine where we will go. Finally, we need to speak the Word out loud to the dark spiritual realm. This is a spiritual battle and words are the weapons we use. The spoken word helps cement our focus on God and the spoken word defeats the enemy.

God is the eternal optimist.

The pessimists of the world have established their destination through their words and their focus. God is the eternal optimist. He believes in us so much that He is willing to invest His Holy Spirit right into our person to give us all we need for victory. Why would He make that kind of investment if He didn't believe in us?

Armed with a new vision coming out of the Word of God and empowered by the presence of the Holy Spirit, the person has all He needs to overcome the law of sin and death. But it is still his choice. At any point, he can turn back. At any point, he can give in to the temptation of the enemy. At any point, he can substitute the religious works of good flesh for true connectedness. At any point, he can sell out on his responsibility to rule and reign, and lay down and wait for God to deliver Him.

God does deliver the truly bound or they could never connect with His presence. Where there are strongholds in the recognition, repentance, releasing, receiving, or renouncing areas, there is usually the need for an intercessor. Outside deliverance is needed. Once the person is at the ruling stage, only minimal help can be given. It is up to the person to say "Amen" and complete the download. It is up to the person to train his gaze upon the godly. No one on the outside can do these tasks for another person—"If by the Spirit, *you* put to death the deeds of the body, you will live" (Rom. 8:13, emphasis added).

The "You" Responsibility

I see many who lose it at this last stage. It is relatively easy to get a person to a point of experiencing the presence of God. It is a much greater challenge to get them to exercise the "you put to death" sentiment of Romans 8:13. After all, the intercessor has been a constant companion and a midwife for the rest of the process. Why should the person be left alone now? Of course we do not leave the person alone. We pray. We give them an understanding of the "you" responsibility. We empower them with Scriptures. We give them a possible vision of how God wants to use them and work through them. We encourage them with the truth that it is God who has started the work (see Philippians 1:6), and it is God who will be right there to empower them to His finish. And then we wait.

The first time the person fails, he may be back for help or he may hide. Failure will come, because it is part of the process of spiritual weightlifting. In basketball, no one starts out hitting every basket he shoots. No one ends up hitting every basket he shoots, either. The goal of a basketball player is to get better. So too, our goal spiritually is to get better, to become mature, to learn to rule and reign. Missed shots are inevitable, but in spiritual circles a missed shot simply means that I go back through the recognition, repentance, releasing, receiving, and, if need be, renouncing stage to get back to the place of presence. From that place of presence, I am poised for a new result— a result of victory, a result of greater maturity.

Ruling Is About Growth

The ruling and reigning stage is about growth more than it is about failure or success. There is no magic level to be achieved since the character and nature of God is our standard. All of us fail according to that standard, even the most mature saint of God who has ever lived. Only Jesus met the standard. All others died still having room for growth. Even the most holy person to have ever lived could be called a "failure." In Christ, no person is a failure. His death on the cross eliminates that word from our vocabulary. The sin payment of Christ can be immediately accessed at any time by any Christian—or non-Christian who will come to Christ! All failures are wiped out and gone when we return to Him.

But—too many have stopped there. They want their sins removed, but miss the very heart of God to develop a mature, ruling, and reigning saint of God, who is transformed into the very character and nature of God. The one who merely wipes out his failures misses the very purpose of God who wants children transformed into His image.

This does seem to be the hardest step for people to take, but it is the most rewarding. It is the embodiment of God's will for us. Without this step, all the work of the previous steps becomes as a vapor, almost as if it had never happened. It is comparable to something a person would access on the Internet, but then choose to discard. It has no permanent influence. Unfortunately, too many today rejoice in having had "an experience" with God. They think they are OK, and headed to heaven because of an experience. The parable of the sower and the seed would seem to indicate otherwise. Only the fourth seed bears fruit; only the fourth seed is commended by God.

Influencing Others

This is also the most rewarding step because it moves us from being nurtured and protected by others, to becoming a nurturer. This is a hard step, to move from being a spiritual child to a spiritual parent, but it is an exciting step. It is moving from being fruit to producing fruit. It is moving from receiving life to giving life.

The purpose of ruling and reigning is not just for self. God has given us an ability to impact others. Biblical ruling that extends beyond self is best described as influence. It is not a controlling or debasing influence. That is demonic ruling. The mature man of God reigns over his own sin nature and provides a covering for others. By exercising his influence, he helps them develop good patterns in their life so that it will be easier for them to eventually say their "Amen" to God. The godly man does not try to lord it over others, because he knows that godliness eventually must come out of a heart choice. He can help establish good patterns, but only the individual can embrace Christ.

7. Resting

There is a final stage that the Bible describes as resting. This is not resting as we think of resting. The person who is "resting" may be hard at work, and may even be in the middle of spiritual warfare. So what is rest?

Ephesians 6 describes the role of the believer in spiritual warfare multiple times as "standing." The believer is to put on the armor of God, to face the battle with quietness and confidence knowing that the Lord is with Him. Having done all, we stand. We do not yell or scream. We don't go chasing after battles. We don't count our weapons. We stand, confident, knowing we are where we need to be—right in the center of the will of God; intimate with God. This is stage five on the life cycle.

Hebrews 4:11 highlights the seeming contradiction of biblical rest: "Let us therefore be diligent to enter that rest, lest anyone fall according to the same example of disobedience." Biblical rest is a place where we must be diligent, but yet we rest. Our diligence is to stay attentive to God. Our diligence is to obey God in a timely manner. But there is a huge difference between human effort (good flesh) and God-empowered effort. When we are in the middle of the will of God, doing His work in His way and in His time, God calls it rest.

It is standing in faith after the activity in the ruling step has been completed. For the mature, it is not even a separate step, but a manner of walking through each of the other steps. There is a time to recognize, to repent, to release, to receive, to renounce, and to rule; and every one of them is done through the empowering work of the Holy Spirit. When human effort perfectly couples with God's empowering, we enter into His rest.

Spiritual Midwives

To see the greatest amount of fruit, the intercessor must operate in the rest of God. We are midwives helping the birthing process. We are not having the baby. We did not create the baby. We nurture what is happening between God and a person, and it is an incredible new creation. It is something very special with great potential. We cannot create it. We can only help the process along if we learn how to assist, how to be a positive influence.

Understanding the seven R's (recognition, repenting, releasing, receiving, renouncing, ruling, and resting) can bring wisdom to the intercessor, but being a good intercessor is more about seeing what God is doing than it is creating a work in a person. We cooperate with the work of God in others. We point them to Him. We call their attention to His work that is already happening. We marvel at the work that He is birthing in them. We explain to them what is happening. We rejoice with them. We rest in His work.

The seven R's are not a process to be applied to a person, or steps to walk a person through. They are a description of the way God works in a person's life. The wise intercessor will learn to recognize where the person is in life and respond accordingly. We are midwives of the Spirit. God is the one who knows the diamond-like character and nature that He has planned for the individual. All we typically see is a body in front of us.

In 2 Corinthian 5:16, we are cautioned against seeing people with our natural eyes, "So stop evaluating Christians by what the world thinks about them or by what they seem to be like on the outside. Once I mistakenly thought of Christ that way, merely as a human being like myself. How differently I feel now!" (TLB).

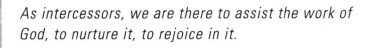

As intercessors, we are there to assist the work of God, to nurture it, to rejoice in it.

When we stop evaluating people according to what we see and start seeing what God wants to do in them, then we release the power of God to bring about 2 Corinthians 5:17, "Therefore, if anyone is in Christ, he is a new creation; old things have passed away; behold, all things have become new." The work of God in a person is truly a new creation. We traditionally have thought of applying this verse to when a person is born again, and it does apply to that. However, every work that brings maturity or transformation into the image of Christ is a new and precious work of the Spirit.

The religions of the world tell us we have the power to become like God through a mere philosophy, a kind of self-created change in behavior. Christianity teaches that only the work of God, embraced by and established in the heart of the individual, will bring true and lasting change. As intercessors, we cannot forget that difference. We are there to assist the work of God, to nurture it, to rejoice in it. Too often we lose track of the One who is at work and try to take over the work ourselves. Or we place all the responsibility squarely on an individual and try to force a person to make a choice to create a work.

Hezekiah panicked. He had begun to think that maybe all of his life of serving God had been for nothing. He needed a midwife and Isaiah was there. God intervened and Hezekiah and a nation took a step forward in Him. Even the great men of God need a greater level of maturity to handle the greater challenges. Greatness in God is grown one step at a time through connection and with the cooperation of the individual in ruling and reigning. All of us have the potential for greatness if we only learn to rule and then rest in Him.

May God give us the eyes to see Him and nurture His life both in us and in others. God, teach us to be spiritual midwives.

God, I realize that one of the greatest signs of Your strength in me is my ability to rest in You. Teach me to rule over my own heart and to cleanse myself before You with Your help, so that I can rule and rest in You. Thank You for the self-control that is found in You. Amen. (Prayer based on Proverbs 16:32; Galatians 5:23.)

Study Guide

1. What does this chapter say is a primary tactic of the devil? When we consider Satan's method of operation, why does that make the ruling stage absolutely vital?

2. What is the purpose God has for our lives? How do these final two R's complete the very purpose God has for our lives?

3. Where is the first place that a person should target his ability to rule? How does a person extend that rule beyond that place?

4. What is the "You" role in ruling? What must the person do himself? What is he not able to do?

5. What role does the Word of God play in this process? What can we do to increase the effectiveness of the Word to help us rule?

6. Those who rule well and enter into rest are actually growing in maturity in Christ. What are some skills that the mature must master to maintain their strength in the midst of challenges?

7. Do you find yourself growing through a receiving model, or have you been more into a works model? What can you do to maximize your growth by walking in more of a connected to God and faith model?

Chapter 17

SHAPING HEARTS

I was absolutely determined not to be beaten. I was like that. I loved to take on the impossible challenges. Tell me something couldn't be done, and it was best to get out of the way. There are times when that quality has actually been an asset, and then there was Joni.

Shaping a heart is not like shaping a clay pot. Clay pots don't talk back to their creators. When people become projects, when they become a task to be conquered, the chances of success take a nosedive. Joni was a project for me. I was armed with a new theology and some successes in the inner healing area. I had experienced a spiritual release personally and had begun to have some success in ministering life to others.

That was when I met Joni. The irresistible force met the immovable object. In this case, the irresistible force lost. But it was part of my training. People cannot become objects or projects. They cannot be an "impossible" challenge to conquer. Attitudes like that are all but guaranteed to cause us to fail in ministry. Why?

There are two reasons. First of all, the flow of the Spirit of God is released through the humble, not the headstrong. One of the most needed lessons for me was that I could not do it. I had to fail multiple times to begin to realize that this thing called ministry was not about me. It was not a content of material to be learned and applied. It was not about knowledge or talent. It was about learning to allow the Spirit of God to touch lives. And that wouldn't happen, unless or until, I got out of the way.

Ministry Is Not a "Project"

Over the years, I have learned that the best posture to go into a ministry situation is to start from the point of view that "I don't have a clue." I frequently find myself well into a situation, still baffled. I sometimes even end a session baffled. If the Spirit doesn't speak or guide, I am much better about refraining from speaking than I used to be. With a much greater dependence on the Spirit, the number of changed lives has gone up significantly. I had to learn that it is not about me, and that I don't have the answers. Every person is unique. No two situations are alike. No set of principles will answer the problem. We are dealing with people, not projects.

Second is the whole concept of ministry through connecting. When I am working on a project, I am above. The project is beneath. There are few things that close the spirit of a person like when we put him under our feet. A project can immediately sense that we are taking on a role of being better than him. That doesn't work. The spirit of the person who is a project shuts off any level of connecting, and all but guarantees failure.

It was like that with Joni, but I didn't have a clue of the dynamics. Joni was hostile. She had no friends. Her family had disowned her. There was one Christian family who was reaching out to her, whether as a project or out of genuine compassion I don't know. With my makeup, it would have been difficult not to make Joni a project. She was obviously on an inferior level with very little going for her. I was bound and determined to help her.

What blew me away was that the more I helped her, the angrier she got. I was giving her some of the best counsel and ministry I had ever given, or so I thought. And she got angrier, and angrier, and angrier. Oh, there were some temporary victories in the midst of ministry to her, but this woman was a perfect example of someone who hated most those who helped her the most. She actually did single out for injury just about anyone who had ever helped her. I did say hostile; and she had no friends. There was a reason.

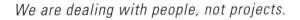

We are dealing with people, not projects.

Looking back, I can see times of desperation where Joni was open to help, but the help always seemed to make her feel like she was in a dead-end position. She desperately needed relationship, but very few had seen enough of their own dark side to step down into the pit with her and treat her as an equal, to take her hand and say, "Come on. Let's walk together." Even if someone had taken that posture, I'm not sure that Joni would have been able to realize that someone was genuinely in the pit with her. I know I didn't go there. I thought I had some answers. I didn't know enough to know that apart from God, I had no answers, just presumptions. To me, she was a project. And I lost.

The same principle comes in to play in the way spiritual headship is often taught. The man is above, the woman is beneath. He is the head. She is the tail. Is it any wonder that many marriages struggle when we teach this kind of posture? God has given the man headship, which is a kind of covering influence over the family. The man is to take his level of influence seriously, but the greatest influence comes when the man steps out of his lofty position.

When a husband or father gets off the pedestal and connects with his wife and children, they will listen. If they listen, he truly has authority. If they don't, what authority does he have? If his only authority is through intimidation and domination, does he have any true authority? The best way to gain authority is to lose the high and mighty status and become a servant. Those who have to appeal to their authority position to maintain authority have minimal influence and definitely lack connecting influence.

Connecting vs. Giving Advice

Connecting requires two persons with an open spirit. The person in a one up position may think of himself as being open, but he seldom is.

Arrogance is never open to connecting. It is too busy fixing. Fixing is not connecting. Releasing the life of God in another person requires learning to be an influence and not a god. Some husbands try to be a god to their families instead of being an influence and a servant. Sure there are times when those in authority have to take functional authority. We live in a fallen world. But most authority should be exercised through relationship and not through demand.

Many counselors take the one up position from the start. I have learned that I have no answers unless God speaks. When I forget this lesson, I almost always get a new chance to learn again. Arrogance closes the spirit of others and shuts down success in ministry. Those sensitive to the spirit of another person will quickly realize when there has been no connection with the other person, merely a passing of advice. To be a lifegiver requires a transfer of life, godly presence, and godly substance. That cannot happen without a level of connectedness. Most people settle for giving advice and hope it works. They think the other person is inferior if it doesn't fix the situation because it "worked for me."

God calls us not just to pass life to another, but to walk with them and to nurture that life until the person is raised up to a point of being able to walk alone. We are to connect and keep connecting until the person is strong enough to keep going. That is the nurturing role of a father. To stand on the outside and give advice or to make demands is arrogance and lacks the nurture needed to bring success.

We are to be lifegivers, not advice givers.

I believe this is what the Scriptures call provoking our children to wrath. (See Ephesians 6:4.) We provoke another person by placing demands on him that he is not capable of meeting. We are to lifegivers, not advice givers. Again, don't take what I am saying to an extreme. In the real world, there are times when people truly want advice. We need to share knowledge with each other. But a broken person needs life, not just advice. And we need to do our best to look someone eye to eye, not from a position of master to child.

Several years ago, I was meditating on the verse from Matthew 7:6 which says, "Do not give what is holy to the dogs; nor cast your pearls before swine, lest they trample them under their feet, and turn and tear you in pieces." Initially when I saw this verse, I began to ask myself why God would refer to a person as a "dog" or a "swine." He doesn't. We are the ones who turn people into something less than human. We are the ones who write people off and declare them to be not worthy of our ministry.

Connection Must Have Compassion

When a Gentile woman comes to Jesus in Matthew 15, it almost seems as if Jesus is calling her a dog. I think that Jesus is actually teaching a lesson to His disciples. They didn't even want Him to talk to her, but wanted Him to send her away. He responds by saying to the woman, "It is not good to take the children's bread and throw it to the little dogs" (Matt. 15:26). Jesus is not putting down the woman, but is quoting the thinking of the Jewish culture. This woman, whom the disciples have written off, responds with humility and faith. Jesus then declares that she has "great faith" and heals her daughter.

The Gentiles were dogs in the eyes of the Jews, but not in the eyes of Jesus. This woman was a human being. Her daughter mattered to Him. Certainly this passage points out that His primary focus was Israel. We all have to know the direction of our mission. We cannot run in ten directions. But the woman mattered to Jesus or He would not have healed her. And it was a great lesson for His disciples.

People are only dogs when we make them dogs. I actually think that is part of the point of the passage in Matthew 7:6. It is foolish for us to even try to think of ministering to a person, especially if that ministry involves some sort of correction, when we are at a point of having judged another person to be a dog. That person will sense the substance of our heart. He will know that we do not value him, and he will despise anything we have to offer.

People are only dogs when we make them dogs.

Before ever reaching out in ministry, the lifegiver needs to ask himself, "Is my heart soft toward this person? Is there a sense of compassion or a sense of superiority?" If there is no compassion, it is best to keep our mouths shut. If there is no compassion, the person is a dog or swine to us and likely will turn and trample us, even as Joni turned on me the more I tried to help her. We cannot be a lifegiver without connection and compassion.

Rescuer or Lifegiver?

When I took on Joni as a project, I turned her into a dog. I didn't know I had turned her into a dog. I thought I was doing the loving and "Christian" thing. This is a great spiritual picture of the rescuer. A rescuer helps people from a one up position. He helps others because he has a big heart—or so he thinks. What he doesn't realize is that he is making them dogs beneath his feet. His big hearted-ness is nothing but an attempt to build his own ego. Most rescuers have that problem. They need to rescue others to feed their own ego. They are not rescuing out of compassion so much as they are being selfish. Worse yet, they don't see the selfishness of it all. They are self-deceived.

As a lifegiver, my goal is very simple: to see the uniqueness of each created person and to do all I can to help each person live in the image of the person whom God created him to be. Every negative and grotesque aspect of a person is a part of his potential gone bad. One with a critical, vengeful spirit has the potential to be a discerning and thinking individual, who is willing to fight for good. The greater the potential for good, the greater the potential for evil. Potential is potential.

We need to realize that every human being is capable of housing godly presence—and not just a carbon copy of God, but a uniquely created manifestation of His presence. This is a presence that no other person could duplicate. When we realize this fact, people begin to mean something—even disabled people who seem to have no "practical" value. Every person has value as a potential vessel to carry the very presence and image of God. What could be a greater value?

The person near death, almost completely incapacitated, is still capable of housing God's presence and presenting His image to the world. Many display very little of God's image because the sin nature has taken over, but if the person had walked with God, His presence would be manifesting all the way to the last breath. The capability of manifesting the presence and image of Christ is our greatest value. Nothing can ever take that away from us—except sin and the sin nature written upon our hearts.

People have value. Even the most grotesque sinner is a potential candidate for reflecting the image of God. The transforming power of the cross is able to break the power of sin and death in a person's life. No person is beyond hope, especially if there is an intercessor who will choose to believe in the value of the person, an intercessor who can begin to give the person a vision for his created purpose.

Understanding this begins to enable us to value another person. If the other person has any openness of spirit at all, the vision within our hearts will begin to penetrate that other person through our words and the touch of the Holy Spirit through us. We then add to vision the spiritual authority that is released through our faith, a faith that is stirred up within us because we are laying hold of the purpose of God for that other person. Mix all of this together and we are beginning to operate with the Spirit's authority to make a difference.

Offer Godly Influence, Not Solutions

Again, the other person has to be open. He has to accept our spiritual presence of faith, vision, and value into his spirit. He also has to chew on it long enough to determine whether or not it is a temporary picture on the screen or a permanent download to be saved. I can offer the life that God has put within me. I can influence, but I cannot bring change. This too is a part of the humility needed to minister. We have to know that ultimately we cannot fix a person or situation.

We can only offer what we have, and we only have something to offer if and when God provides it.

Ministry is not like shaping a clay pot. It is a complex and interactive mission of shaping a human heart. We must get the permission of the heart to change the heart. In one way, it is like shaping a clay pot. We can fire off in negative ways and harden the pot prematurely or we can walk in the compassion of God and continue to fashion more beauty into the pot—of course with the pots permission.

I didn't understand this at the time I was ministering to Joni. To this day, I wonder if the outcome could have been different if I had known what I know now. She went through a number of years of serious struggle and of being left in almost total isolation before God began to break through to her heart. The good news is that God never stopped reaching out to Joni. I may not have been effective, but that didn't keep God from reaching her. He gives us the opportunity to participate with Him in His work of redemption, but His success or failure is not limited to us. If we prepare ourselves and become an effective tool in His hand, He will use us. If not, He will search for other ways to reach the heart of the one who is seeking Him.

The Joni's of the world are crying for someone to connect with them. They want someone who can look at them with the Father's eyes and see something of value. God wants to release His life into them and through them. Are you willing to do what is needed to shape hearts in a way that God's life can flow? The harvest is plentiful, but the laborers are few. (See Matthew 9:37.) I pray that you will hear God's call to become one who releases God's life in and through others.

> *Father God, I recognize that I am a piece of clay in Your hands. Do with me as You desire. Mold me. Shape me. And use me as one who will help mold others into Your image. Give me Your eyes to believe, Your hands to shape, and Your heart to pray that I might truly see Your life activated in me and released in and through others. (Prayer based on Jeremiah 18:4, 29:11–13.)*

Study Guide

1. Why does making a person a project shut down any hope for success?

2. How does a person with true spiritual headship actually add to his authority and influence?

3. When Jesus appears to be calling a Gentile woman a dog, what is He actually doing? How can understanding the "dog" concept help us in ministering to others?

4. How does the chapter say that we provoke another person to wrath? How do we keep from doing this?

5. What is the difference between a rescuer and a true lifegiver? In your own experience, how can you tell the difference between helping when you "need to help" from when God is motivating you to help?

6. How do we learn to value others? What are the ingredients that bring life to others?

7. As you have ministered to others, what kinds of ego protection tendencies do you have? How do the Joni's of this world get to you and cause you to slide into the flesh? What do you need to do to overcome those tendencies and learn to release the life of God in others?

FROM NEGATIVE TO POSITIVE IN DETAIL

For those wanting a more detailed list, below is a list of the godly potentials that correspond with twenty-one sin areas. The purpose of this list is to help the lifegiver think transformation. It is not good to dwell on the sin area that has taken a person captive. It is much better to meditate on the person God wants him to be and on how to get there. Use this list to help develop your vision and value for those to whom you are ministering. The list is in groups of three. Each of the three are in the same basic spiritual flow as the first term listed of the three.

Sin Area: Core Value and Possible Potential

1. Pride: A desire to lead others, to give direction, nurture to others

2. Jealousy: Ability to see the gifting in others, to honor

3. Rejection, self-pity: Willing to sacrifice for or work to earn the respect of others

4. Fear, cowardice: Ability to submit to or surrender to God and others

5. Unbelief, worry: Faith, ability to visualize

6. No self-control: Spontaneity, flexibility

7. Rebellion: Creativity, independent, bold, courageous

8. Witchcraft: Sensitivity to the spiritual realm, desire for power

9. Liar: Can see subtleties, willing to match wits

10. Lust, self-indulgence: Value contentment, friendship, being at peace, comfortable

11. Materialism: Appreciation for and proper use of things

12. Stealing, laziness: Creativity, ability to maximize efforts toward productivity

13. Bitterness: Love, valuing of relationship, compassion

14. Anger: Emotional support, motivator, zeal

15. Self-hatred: Ability to see self honestly, to see good and bad, humility

16. Critical spirit: Discernment, love of truth, detailed understanding

17. Gossip: Desire to proclaim knowledge, to use it to motivate others

18. Quarreler: Values uniqueness of a point of view, insightful

19. Selfish ambition: single minded focus, directed toward a goal, self-control

20. Intimidation, unclean speech: Supervision and control, using language to motivate others

21. Perfectionism: Attention to detail, industrious, desire for excellence

NOTES

Chapter 4
Making Sense of Life

1. *Vine's Expository Dictionary of New Testament Words* lists two primary definitions for the Greek word *thanatos*. Both definition 1 and 2 cite the idea of separation. The first definition cites a separation of the soul from the body, and the second speaks of the separation of man from God

Chapter 13
Weighting for God

1. *Strong's Exhaustive Concordance of the Bible*, James Strong, 1890. The word *glory* comes from the root of Strong's OT:3513. The root is transliterated kabad (kaw-bad'); or kabed (kaw-bade'). It is a primitive root meaning to be heavy, i.e. in a bad sense (burdensome, severe, dull) or in a good sense (numerous, rich, honorable; causatively, to make weighty [in the same two senses]).

ABOUT THE AUTHOR

David Case is the founder and current President of Live Free Ministries, a ministry dedicated to nurturing the presence and power of Christ's life in the church and in its leaders. With the increasing dysfunctions of today's world, David believes that the church should shine as a light with hope and healing for those that the world's system have not been able to help. Instead, too often, we find ourselves referring the "difficult" cases to the world system for help.

The gospel has the power to change lives and that has been the heartbeat of much of David's ministry. In the early 1990s, he began holding retreats for both pastors and laypersons, helping them break through bondages and pointing them toward fulfilling the call of God on their lives. Over the last eighteen years, he has been growing in his ability to communicate the message of how to bring restoration to people through a spiritual model. While those early retreats had great success in ministering individually to the hurting, David is now targeting ways to communicate this method and message on a much larger scale.

Having pastored the same church for eighteen years, one of his targets is to give other pastors the tools they need to implement the lifegiver model into a whole church setting. Of course, one of the keys to this is to develop individuals to see and understand a spiritual model of life, and to be able to apply that model at an individual level to walk in freedom and fullness of life.

In addition to being an author, David co-hosts a radio program, has ministered internationally, and is also experienced in very practical settings of teaching and administration in a school setting. This variety of experiences brings a blend that gives him the ability to be very versatile and adaptable to many different applications. It is his heart to blend the supernatural of the spiritual realm with a very solid application in the natural realm.

In *Releasing God's Life*, you will get the chance to see that variety of experiences and to experience new insights into how you function and also into how to minister to others. It is truly David's hope, that through this book, you might be more effectively equipped to bring healing and restoration to a hurting and dying world.